FROM IMAGE TO LIKENESS

FROM IMAGE TO LIKENESS

The Christian Journey
into God

William A. Simpson

CONTINUUM • NEW YORK

1997

The Continuum Publishing Company
370 Lexington Avenue
New York, NY 10017

Copyright © 1997 by William A. Simpson

Printed in the United States of America

Library of Congress Cataloging-in-Publication Data
Simpson, William A., 1962-
 From image to likeness: the Christian journey into God / William
A. Simpson.
  p. cm.
 ISBN 0-8264-1016-2
 1. Mysticism. 2. Spiritual life— Catholic Church. 3. Catholic
Church—Doctrines. I. Title.
BV5083.S56 1997
248.2—dc21   96-47833
                                                        CIP

Beloved, we are God's children now;
what we will be has not yet been revealed.
What we do know is this: when he is revealed,
we will be like him, for we will see him as he is.

1 John 3.2

Contents

Acknowledgments

A great many people are involved in making a book. I am particularly grateful to Reverend Bob Fowler, pastor of Saint James Methodist Church in Central City, Colorado, and Father John Wengrovius, rector of Calvary Episcopal Church in Golden, Colorado. Both clergymen generously agreed to read and comment upon each chapter of this book as I wrote it. Their many years of pastoral experience helped me make *From Image to Likeness* a much better book. I am grateful to Peggy Murray and Julie Wahtola who read and commented on the complete manuscript. I would also like to thank Christopher Shields, George Bealer, Mark Tanzer, Tom Beckwith, Brother Benito Williamson, O.C.S.O., and Father William Meninger, O.C.S.O. with whom I discussed many of the ideas in this book. I am grateful to Frank Oveis of Continuum for his help preparing this book for publication. Finally, I would like to thank Barbara Goodrich, my wife, for her love and support during this project.

Foreword

This is a great little book! You are fortunate to be holding it in your hands. Don't put it down. Read it. The author comes out of a solid Christian, monastic, and academic background. But he really comes *out of it*. Using his formative monastic experience and his rich academic foundations, William Simpson adapts the principles of the monastic journey to daily life "in the world." A clear and simple style reveals a profound message. You will be led from the Gospel of St. John to the Denver Botanical Gardens, from Clement of Alexandria to C. S. Lewis, from the desert fathers to the author's kitchen in Golden, Colorado.

In many ways this little book follows in the footsteps of Evelyn Underhill, doing for the end of the twentieth century what she did for the beginning of it. He presents the search for God (the fruit of a union which begins even before the search) as a call given to everyone. It is possible to pursue it guided by the classical Christian tradition while being, at the same time, free from many of its "hang-ups."

According to the author, there is nothing exclusive or extraordinary about the journey toward God. In a mystical conversion, "the business at hand is not so much to affirm a set of propositions about God but to begin a friendship with God." With a freshness, a sense of humor, and a clarity of style, he brings out of his storeroom things old and new. "God wishes," he says in chapter 3, "to visit us in our time and he will restore us to his likeness within the context of our own lives." Enjoy!

William Meninger, O.C.S.O.

9

Chapter 1

From Image to Likeness

As iron at a distance is drawn by the loadstone, there being some invisible communications between them, so is there in us a world of Love to somewhat, though we know not what in the world that should be.
—Thomas Traherne, *Centuries*, I.2

Growing into the Divine Likeness

This spring I planted seven dwarf fruit trees in our garden. I set them out in a hexagonal pattern hoping to make the best use of the space available in the plot. Each tree is at least eleven feet from its neighbor, the minimum spacing required in a successful planting. In the center of the hexagon I planted a self-pollinating sweet cherry. Around it I planted two types of Japanese plums, an apple, an apricot, a persimmon, and an oriental pear. The apple will pollinate with the tree across the creek, and the oriental pear will pollinate with the pears my wife Barbara and I planted last spring. The persimmon and apricot are self-sufficient. I have not yet seen my trees bloom or bear fruit. As Saint John would have said, what they are yet to be has not yet come to light (see 1 John 3.2).

To a greater or lesser extent, I suppose that each of us is like my new orchard. We are not yet what we have it in us to be. Some of my friends are well along in the Christian life and so are very much themselves. I suspect that you would get a fairly clear idea of what Christ is like by having a conversation with one of these nearly-grown Christians. Others of us are still beginners. We carry around all the hope and promise of our true natures, but what we really are is not yet manifest. As the medieval mystics liked to say, we bear the image of Christ but have not yet grown into his likeness.

This book is about how Christians have traditionally understood and practiced the process of growing into the divine likeness. It is a book about mysticism, that is, the art of becoming one with God. Yet since it is a book about *Christian* mysticism, I will have as much to say about growth in love of God and neighbor as I will about the sorts of inward experiences which often accompany such growth. I have no secrets to tell. As Saint Augustine once said, God created us for himself, and our hearts are restless until they rest in him. The Christian journey into God consists in coming again to God's embrace and knowing it as if for the first time. Consequently, there is nothing exclusive or esoteric about the Christian mystical journey. It is what any maturing child of God might expect.

The Christian mystic seeks oneness with Christ through an inner search for his or her true nature. The central feature of our true natures is that we are creatures made in God's image, that is, created to love God and to see and love the world as God sees and loves it. In our perfected state, we will not differ from God in our most basic stance toward creation but only in the scope and intensity of our love for it. All the other properties by which we mark our distinctness from God are essentially facts about our inability to love all that exists to the extent that God loves it. For example, the banal truth that no human being is all-good, all-loving, or all-powerful really means that not one of us can love everything as thoroughly as God does. While fully grown Christians can and do regard each creature they encounter with wonder and respect, only God can love all things, individually, in an instant. The fact that we are finite and God infinite is no reason to be discouraged. One of the great pleasures of the Christian life is to turn a corner and glimpse something new about God. Our finitude ensures that we will continue to be surprised.

Love Divine

Although our powers of loving are limited, they can still be godlike. Our love can have the same quality as God's even though it may lack its scope. When Barbara wants to tune her harp, she strikes the heel of her hand with a tuning fork and then brings the harp string up to that pitch. Once tuned, the string will resonate at the same frequency as the tuning fork. If I had the ear for it, I would say that both the harp string and the tuning fork play the same middle-C. Although the materials and the structures of the harp and tuning fork differ, Barbara hears the same note. Similarly, if you or I manage just a scintilla of Christian charity, we will manifest one and the same divine love. Although our love will differ from God's in its scope and intensity, it will not differ in its intrinsic, divine quality.

So far, I have been speaking of Christian charity in general terms. I have told you that the Christian mystic achieves union with God through it, but I have not been specific about what *it* is. Let us begin with how the New Testament speaks of love. The Greek word for Christian love is *agape*. It comes from the same root as the Greek words for holiness, awe, and delight. When Saint Paul tells us that three things, faith, hope, and love, endure and that the greatest of these is love, he is using the word *agape* (see 1 Corinthians 13.13). Similarly, the Greek word for "saint" or "holy person," *hagios*, shares this root meaning. After all, a saint is someone who delights in God and in what God has made and elicits that same delight in other people.

Agape is not a mere synonym for "self-sacrifice." Certainly love will draw us toward selfless acts, but these will be a byproduct of a more basic orientation. At its root, Christian love consists in seeing all things, including oneself, as elegant, delightful, and full of wonders. This is how God sees you and me and everything else that exists, and as we come to share his love we will see things this way too. There is no room for glowering, grudging self-sacrifice here. As Saint Paul puts it: "If I give away all my possessions, and if I hand over my body so that I may boast, but do not have love, I gain nothing" (1 Corinthians 13.3). *Agape* does not denote other good things such as sexual attraction, friendship, or the affection members of a rugby team have for one another. The Greeks had other words for these relationships. Yet because Christian love consists in a new way of seeing God, other people, and the rest of creation, it readily encompasses husbands and wives, friends, and colleagues.

Grace and Conversion

We do not discover divine love by our own devices. The process begins with grace and continues as we respond to grace. Grace is God's way of introducing himself to us, and the divine greeting comes with no preconditions or subsequent duties. At some point each of us experiences God's love, and we may or may not allow ourselves to be caught up in it. True, Christ sent the apostles out to fish for souls, but, unlike fish, Christians choose to be caught. Once caught, a Christian's life will consist in ongoing, willing cooperation with freely given grace. Like a seedling in a garden, Christian love grows and is guided by its own inner workings. We can cultivate the soil it grows in and clear weeds from around it, but there is always something gratuitous about love's development within us. This is because God himself is at work. Lived Christianity consists in a first-person encounter with God. It is a lifelong adventure, and to expect anything less underestimates God's tenacity and one's own potential to live a rich and robustly human life.

Sometimes, of course, the presence of God is difficult to discern in one's life. Yet this does not mean that God has abandoned us or suddenly ceased to exist. Rather, it is quite reasonable for us to assume that God is now working in us in a new way. The personal relationship continues; God is just behaving more subtly. A monk much more attuned to this than I once took a picture of a hook and pulley dangling out of a hayloft. In the photo you can only see the rope, the pulley, the hook, and the empty sky. He liked to joke that it was the only known photograph of God. Such is divine grace. It is present even when we cannot discern its origin or goal.

Once we assent to grace our lives subtly but irrevocably change. The external conditions of one's life will most likely remain unaltered. One's appearance, surroundings, or bank balance will not change. One will remain, say, a nondescript man with thick glasses. What does change is one's entire way of perceiving God, oneself, other people, and everything else. Quite suddenly, everything appears fresh and infused with wonders. For the first time we take to heart a fact we already knew: that God created and sustains the world.

I began wearing glasses in my early teens. The first time I looked through my new lenses my breath caught in my throat for a second. Abruptly I found myself in a new universe. For the first time I could see the twigs on the cottonwoods and my father's pupils across the dinner table. Something similar happens when we first acquiesce to grace. Quite unexpectedly, we glimpse everything from God's perspective, and in a very real sense we see things for the first time. Traditionally, mystics have referred to this first assent to God's love and the accompanying change in perception as conversion.

But the word "conversion" can be misleading. In the first place, conversion isn't about getting religion. Conversion is not about affirming a set of doctrines about God so much as it is the discovery of the full import of what one already believes. Those undergoing conversion experience a new awareness of God's love and the possibilities available to one caught up in it. Conversion presupposes religious faith but posits a wider scope of religious experiences. The mystic who suddenly converts from atheist to Anglican or from Buddhist to Baptist is a bit of an odd duck since the crucial features of conversion are experiential rather than doctrinal. A more typical trajectory would be from lukewarm Baptist to committed Christian or from cultural Buddhist to sincere seeker of enlightenment. In mystical conversion, the business at hand is not to affirm a set of propositions about God but to begin a friendship with God.

Faith, Hope, and Charity

Conversion marks a passage from belief into faith. Mere belief turns on affirming propositions and has little to do with holiness. For instance, if I told you that I sincerely believed that the City of Golden would not forget to send me this month's water bill, I would not expect any complements on my character. On the other hand, if someone were to tell me about her trust in her husband, I would take it as a mark of her love for him. This is a weightier matter. The trust one has for a spouse or a good friend goes beyond simply believing good things about that person. Rather than loving those dear to us because of what we believe about them, we have faith in them because we already love them.

As the letter to the Hebrews puts it, faith is "the assurance of things hoped for [and] the conviction of things not seen" (Hebrews 11.1). The writer's claim is that faith undergirds hope because faith begins in love. Love consists in a relationship between the lover and the beloved, and it is in this respect that love presupposes the content of faith. If I catch a cold, I trust that Barbara will offer to make a pot of soup for me not because of a codicil in our marriage license pertaining to soup making but because we love one another. In fact, a soup making contract would not be evidence of faith and love at all but, rather, of pusillanimity. If faith is to be counted as a virtue it must always involve a capacity for creative goodness rooted in love.

A loving relationship is never static. At our wedding reception I toasted Barbara saying, "May we grow old together, see our children's children, and live in peaceful times." In saying this, I wished us a full and changing life. I wished us a set of adventures through which we would come

to know ourselves and one another more deeply, and I wished
that over the years we would come to love one another more
thoroughly. Love always desires and directs itself toward its
completion. Hope is love's desire to become full-grown.
Hope anticipates love's maturity. This also is what Robert
Browning had in mind in the first lines of *Rabbi Ben Ezra*:

> Grow old along with me!
> The best is yet to be,
> The last of life, for which the first was made:
> Our times are in his hand
> Who saith, 'A whole I planned,
> Youth shows but half; trust God: see all, nor be afraid.'

Those in love with God and with one another are in for a
life-long adventure, and the loving itself will provide much of
that adventure's content. The journey into the divine likeness begins with love, begets faith, and is lived-out in hope.

Circling Up the Wagons

Faith and mystical conversion have little in common
with that peculiar nineteenth century idea that the most
sublime religious act is a blind "leap of faith." Some people
back then thought that faith is most genuine when it is most
unwarranted. For example, should one be disturbed by, say,
Darwinian evolution or inconveniently ancient fossils, one
ought obstinately to reaffirm one's faith in the face of both
reason and the evidence of one's senses. On this view, the
more objectively absurd one's faith the better—for then it is
most truly faith. At its wildest extreme, we find Mark

Twain's Sunday school student who claimed that faith was "believing what you know ain't true." Philosophers of religion call such a position fideism.

Notice that fideism is an attempt to rescue one's religion from the clutches of merely human cleverness. Unfortunately, fideism is not internally consistent. In the first place, fideism presupposes that one is no longer experiencing God's presence and that it is up to the individual to save himself or herself by willing continued belief. This, of course, sets up a peculiar relationship with God because now it is the fideist who gives himself or herself faith. In this respect, fideistic faith is a kind of work. Such belief is no longer a response to grace but a substitute for it. In point of fact, the idea that the sincerity of our religious beliefs is proportional to our lack of evidence for them shifts one's attention from God to the attitudes one entertains about God, and it all ends in a kind of sad self-absorption.

Moreover, if the sincerity of one's faith were proportional to its "blindness," then God would be unable to intervene in our lives without causing us to love him inauthentically. After all, if we began to experience deeper union with God through love, then we would have reason to believe that God existed. But if we had reason to believe that God existed, our faith would not be "genuine" faith but a belief warranted by our experiences. Thus, fideistic faith is possible only given God's apathy or non-existence. So much, then, for fideism and the blind leaps of faith.

Characteristics of Conversion

Unlike fideists, Christian mystics awaken to the ramifications of what they already believe. Through grace we recognize that the world is much larger than we realized. Prior to his or her conversion, the Christian mystic most likely believes in the tenets of the faith and in the possibility of personal experiences of God. After conversion the substance of one's faith takes on a palpable immediacy, and the experience of God's grace is no longer so much abstractly contemplated as actively enjoyed.

Mystics often express this new found awareness of God's love and the possibilities available to one caught up in it as the discovery of a new sense. Many times those who have undergone mystical conversion will say that the "eyes" of their hearts or souls were opened by a loving Father. Others talk about hearing the voice of Christ rather than just hearing about him, and still others prefer to tell of their first taste of the Holy Spirit. In any event, they all seem to be describing a new and direct awareness of God, an awareness which utterly transforms their lives.

Saint Paul and Saint Antony

Sometimes conversion consists in an abrupt break with how one previously regarded the world and lived one's life. The conversion of Saint Paul is the best known example of immediate conversion. According to the Acts of the Apostles, Paul, then a devout Pharisee, experienced a blinding vision of Jesus on the road to Damascus and immediately sought baptism (see Acts 9.1–19). Quite suddenly, Paul's life came into clearer focus as he discovered a new and more wholesome outlet for his talents. Paul would remain a professional holy man, but the nature of his message changed dramatically. Prior to his conversion Paul merely reacted to an extrinsic threat to his orthodox Jewish piety. After his conversion he preached what he had seen that day on the road.

A similarly abrupt change is apparent in the life of Saint Antony the Great. Antony was born in 351 to a devout agricultural family in central Egypt. By his eighteenth birthday both his parents had died, and Antony had inherited about two hundred acres of farm land. For several months Antony's life went on as it had before, shaped by the dual rhythms of the farm and the Sunday liturgy. Yet Antony could not settle into this pattern. He brooded over the old stories about the apostles who abruptly left their fishing boats to follow Jesus (see Mark 1.16–20) or about the first Christians who sold all they had so that the money could be distributed to the poor (see Acts 4.32–37).

It happened one Sunday when Antony was late for church. Antony walked in while the gospel was being read. The lesson for that day was the story of Jesus's advice to a rich young man: "If you wish to be perfect, go, sell your possessions, and give the money to the poor, and you will have treasure in heaven; then come follow me" (Matthew 19.21). It seemed to Antony that the words of the lesson were addressed to him directly. That same day Antony parceled out his farm among his neighbors and slipped off into the desert to be alone with God.

John Wesley

John Wesley (1703–1791) also experienced a sudden conversion, although it took a while to lay the foundations for his abrupt break with the past. Wesley was born to a devout Anglican family in Lincolnshire, England. The son of a priest, Wesley also received holy orders and remained an Anglican for the rest of his life. While a student at Oxford, Wesley founded a group called the Holy Club whose members devoted themselves to a rigorous schedule of prayer and self-edification. Members of the Holy Club were so keen on their methodical, tightly-scripted devotions that their fellow students soon gave them a nickname: Methodists.

As a young priest Wesley traveled to the British North American colony of Georgia where he attempted to impress the local Indians with his brand of high church Anglicanism. Needless to say, his missionary adventure failed, and he returned to London severely disappointed. Then in 1738 Wesley attended a small but fervent Protestant prayer group where Luther's doctrine of justification by faith was being discussed. The notion of generously-given grace turned the founder of the Oxford Holy Club's world inside out. As Wesley later put it, "I felt my heart strangely warmed."

Abruptly, the failed missionary found not only himself but his voice. For the next fifty years he would shuttle among England's mining and mill towns preaching an experience of conversion which he called "the second blessing." For Wesley, the first blessing was the sort of belief he enjoyed before God warmed his heart. This was the religion of Nicene Creed and prayer book piety. In itself, the first blessing was good but incomplete. Wesley's second blessing was the direct awareness God gave him of the scope and possibilities of what he already believed. Quite suddenly, Wesley realized that God was drawing him into an intimate and loving relationship through which he, would be regenerated and eventually perfected.

Gradual Conversion

Mystical conversion need not be instantaneous. Often, one awakens gradually to grace's possibilities. In these cases, mystical conversion generally begins with restlessness and dissatisfaction. One senses something incomplete about his or her life but cannot identify what might be lacking. One feels like a water spider darting about on a deep pond under a clear sky. Though capable of jerky motion across the surface of the pond, the water spider cannot venture into the air above or the water below. Similarly, those in the initial phases of conversion feel themselves skudding about upon the surface of things, never experiencing what might be so near above or below them. Such a state may continue for some months or even years.

To put the matter differently, one might say that the embryonic mystic's personality has yet to unify itself. In the case of young Wesley, the elements of the fully-grown Christian are present, but they have yet to coalesce into a coherently-structured whole. The result is that the self flits about first trying out one of its potentialities and then another, unaware of any overarching pattern. It is not surprising that such people are dissatisfied with their lives and often unsuccessful in bringing others to God. After all, they are not yet able to bring their energies fully to bear upon anything. Since they have yet to discover a focus or mission for their lives, they cannot be expected to give others what they do not yet have themselves.

But God is generous with his grace. At some point the non-unified self experiences God's invitation to greater communion. The Christian mystic responds by looking inward to discern his or her unique way of participating in the divine image. The awakening self does not just feel drawn to God in a new and more intense way. Those experiencing mystical conversion actually experience themselves partaking of God's loving nurture of all that exists. As a result of this new vision one comes to see that selfish concerns and purely personal agendas are at odds with one's true identity as a child of God. One comes to see one's role in the universe as much like a musician playing in a symphony orchestra. One recognizes that one's lifework is a component of a great fugue and not a mere solo performance.

Completing God's Creative Work

Through the experience of conversion mystics realize that their lives are entwined with many other lives, and that a selfish individualism is not so much vulgar as simply false. All creation is fitted to be caught up in God's loving embrace, and to those undergoing conversion anything short of this seems unreal. Unfortunately, one of the great scandals and misfortunes of Christianity is that this new awareness of the scope of divine love has often been interpreted in terms of "unselfing" or the annihilation of personal identity. True, those experiencing conversion no longer view themselves as isolated individuals fighting their way through a hostile world. The reason, however, is not that they lose their personalities or that God drains them of their uniqueness. Rather, they come to see themselves as participants in God's plan for creation and as capable of making a unique contribution to that plan. It is misleading to refer to the Christian mystic's conversion as an "unselfing." Let us be very clear about this point: Christian mystics do not lose themselves in infinite being or some such thing; they find their true selves in Christ.

Oftentimes, a misunderstanding of our Lord's injunction to "deny oneself, take up one's cross, and follow me" (Mark 8.34) has been used to prop up the idea that union with Christ must destroy one's personality and negate one's hopes for the future. Once such an assumption takes hold, even a wholesome desire to live up to one's innate potential may be viewed as selfish. Tragically, this may lead some impressionable people to distrust their natural inclinations and to dampen down their hopes and dreams. But this was never what the Lord had in mind. Notice that in the same breath he says, "For what will it profit them to gain the whole world and forfeit their life?" (Mark 8.36). Christ's point is not that it is a good thing to give up what is essential to us but, rather, that nothing should be placed before our true identities as children of God.

Christians are called to become more themselves, not less so. Last winter I telephoned a monastery to arrange a date for my yearly retreat. Chatting with one of the brothers about the year's news I learned that a benefactor had given the monastery two round trip plane tickets to Israel. The abbot decided to send two of the senior monks off on a pilgrimage, a learned priest and a simple lay brother. The priest was already a seasoned traveler. He was educated at a prestigious European university and had traveled to India to meet with the Dali Lama. The lay brother, by contrast, had entered the monastery in his teens and rarely strayed from the abbey farm. When they returned, the two monks were asked to tell the assembled community about their pilgrimage. The priest told his fellow monks about what it was like to see the ancient sites and mused about how the culture of modern Israel occasionally permits one to glimpse the world of Abraham and Jesus. The priest spoke with an articulate wonder about having been in such places. When his turn came, the lay brother told about the people he met on planes and in airports. He spoke with delight on restaurant menus and the types of sheep grazing on the hills. Yet his report, too, was colored by the same wonder, and it was agreed that both monks had made a successful pilgrimage. Both monks made successful pilgrimages because each man made his own. Each monk brought his own mode of wonder to the journey, and *that*, after all, was the important thing.

Integrity

God wills that each of us become the person he intends us to be. The Christian mystic's guiding insight is that he or she is a child of God intended for unending union with the Trinity in the communion of saints. Everything else is to be measured against this truth. The direct result of such awareness is that what previously seemed important about one's life now seems trivial. One recognizes that it is not of our essence to be taxpayers, honors students, or a company's "human resources." Class, race, reputation, gender, ability, or how one experiences sexual attraction must all take second place to one's status as a child of God among children of God.

What the Christian must steer clear of is the surface static and accidental features of his or her life. This requires a certain amount of applied intelligence. Everything in the world exists because of God's loving sustenance, and, at least to this extent, everything that is is good. When we try to decide which things help and which things hinder our progress toward union with God, we are rarely called to make an explicit choice between good and evil. Usually we find ourselves making choices between greater and lesser goods.

In my own case, I once had the opportunity to become a professor of Greek philosophy. Having completed my Ph.D., I could have taken a series of temporary positions, published a few articles, and after a few years landed a tenure-track job. To achieve this, Barbara and I would have had to be willing to move every couple years and, perhaps, never set down roots even in the community where we finally lighted. Worse, such a career would involve moving hundreds of miles from my parents, and not being readily available to them as they aged. Barbara and I agreed that as an only child I had a special obligation to my parents and that I could not fulfill it well at a distance. Finally, I could not bring myself to leave the community where I grew up and where my family has lived for the past hundred years. The goods of family and community trumped the possible goods of an academic career, and so Barbara and I will grow old together here in Golden.

In any event, conversion leads directly to a set of decisions about how to live a life that is most distinctly one's own. Those undergoing conversion have just begun to sense the true possibilities, scope, and wonder of the Christian faith. They have just glimpsed it in the corners of their eyes. The newly awakened Christian senses that there are many more aspects of God and oneself just out of sight and wants very much to discover them. Then one begins the wholesome labor of the purification of the self in order better to perceive God's presence.

What Lies Ahead

Mystical conversion marks the beginning of a journey into Christian maturity. Having recognized the full import of what one believes, it now becomes imperative to assimilate fully the possibilities available to a creature made in God's image and capable of the divine likeness. Yet just as a few saplings set out in April are not likely to produce a crop in September, having undergone conversion we will probably not find ourselves immediately humming with the divine likeness. Just as young trees need to be tended for several years before they bloom or bear fruit, the human heart must be cultivated for several seasons before it becomes truly fruitful.

In this book I hope to describe some of the territory one might encounter on the journey into the divine likeness. For the sake of clarity, I have adopted a traditional model of the mystical life which portrays the individual passing from *conversion* through *purgation, illumination,* and the *dark night* before arriving at *divine union.* Conversion, as we have seen, consists in one's awakening to the possibilities available to a child of God. However, if these possibilities are to be realized fully, one will usually have to become free of various bad habits, misconceptions, and crippling attachments. The process of purgation begins as one embarks upon this project.

With God's help, one can expect that the purgative way will yield some successes leading to a heightened awareness of God's presence. Now prayer will be a richer experience consisting of fewer words and extended periods of delightful silence. Such is the illuminative way, that phase of the journey toward Christian maturity in which the healthy toil of purgation begins to bear fruit and the inklings of conversion become more explicit. In conversion one delighted in the possibility of regularly experiencing God's presence, and now in the illuminative way this presence is often accessible. This is a sweet but transitory part of the journey.

Imperceptibly at first, clouds begin to form on the periphery of the illuminated consciousness. One might become jaded to the divine presence or even bored at prayer. The divine presence seemingly begins to hide itself, and one may be unable to discern it for a few days at a time. Then the ordeal begins in earnest. The previous sense of intimacy disappears, and one begins to suspect that God has rejected him or her or even that God does not exist after all. The world grows dark and closes in around one. Now one gets a detailed course in suffering, evil, and cruelty. So begins the dark night of the soul, the most harrowing but also the most hallowing phase of the journey into the divine likeness.

When the dark night releases its grip, one walks away changed. The confrontation with the dark mysteries of suffering and evil might nearly have overcome one, but as the clouds lift one finds within oneself a new strength and integrity. Rather than seeing God as a sort of cosmic bellhop who ought to be rushing around seeing to it that everyone is cozy, now one begins to take responsibility for the status of one's own life, for the condition of one's community, and the state of the environment. God is our creator, and as we mature part of sharing in the divine likeness will involve furthering God's creative and sustaining activity.

Map Is Not Territory

The metaphor of a journey from conversion through purgation to divine union makes for a simple map of the soul's ascent to God. A map, however, is not the same thing as the territory it represents, and each soul is its own place. Ultimately, the journey into Christian maturity is something lived rather than learned, and so any book of this type is of only limited value. I cannot cause you to experience God; at best, I can only encourage you to seek God in and for yourself and, perhaps, assure you that you are not alone should your experiences surprise you.

Few journeys into the divine likeness proceed in sync with the phases of mystical development I will describe. Conversion, purgation, illumination, dark night, and union need not be discrete, one-time-only episodes. Some people's lives cycle from one to another of these phases in an upward spiral toward God. For others, there may be an extensive overlap of phases. For instance, someone might be well into the transforming union even though the dark night has yet to release its grip on her. Finally, some phases may be omitted altogether. For example, some people never have a discrete experience of conversion or never experience the dark night. In any case, it is important to have one's own experience of God and not attempt to stuff that experience into one or another of the approved models of how such experiences are supposed to transpire.

Chapter 2

The Land of Unlikeness

Truly there are two worlds. One was made by God, the other by men. That made by God was great and beautiful. Before the fall it was Adam's joy and the Temple of his Glory. That made by man is a Babel of Confusions: Invented Riches, Pomps and Vanities, brought in by Sin. Leave one that you may enjoy the other.
—Thomas Traherne, *Centuries*, I.7

Aelred's Allegory

About eight hundred years ago a British monk named Aelred spun an allegory from the parable of the prodigal son. The parable (Luke 15.11–32) tells of a young man who demanded his inheritance from his father and then squandered it in a faraway land. According to Aelred, the young man represents each of us. Our inheritance from God is his likeness, that is, our capacity to see all creation as God sees it and to love it as God does. All but the most mature of us sense its absence. We find ourselves, says Aelred, in a distant country, a land of unlikeness, mourning the loss of what we could have been.

But Aelred does not conclude the allegory here. In the parable the son comes to his senses and decides to return to his father's house. The father, who seems to have been waiting for his son, recognizes him while he is still a great distance away, and prepares a feast to welcome him. Similarly, says Aelred, God is waiting for us to come to ourselves and return to him, and he can see us even from a great distance. Through the experience of conversion Christian mystics come to themselves and resolve to return to God. The joy accompanying conversion is mixed with an awareness that one has just begun the journey back to God. To return home one must leave the land of unlikeness. Traditionally, this part of the mystical journey is called the *purgative way*.

Unlikeness Is Unreality

What constitutes the land of unlikeness varies from one soul to the next. We may find the land of unlikeness in groups with which we are associated or within the confines of our own minds. We may find ourselves there on account of an organizational culture shot through by secrecy, fear, or selfishness, or we might place ourselves in it by nursing private hatreds, lusts, or ambitions. We may come to the land of unlikeness through a process of attrition in which we become accustomed to being undervalued and so scale back our capacities for faith, hope, and love to the level expected of us. On the other hand, we may forget the importance of cherishing God's creation and so come to regard the world as a mere instrument for getting what we think we need.

In any case, the land of unlikeness has a common feature wherever one finds it: its fundamental unreality. God made us in his image and likeness, and it is not in our nature to be satisfied with anything short of living this out. Each of us can be one with God through love, and we naturally feel dissatisfied when our lives lack such loving union. A friend of mine once said that the greatest repressed desire people have is not for power or sexual release but for union with God. What we really want is to be caught up in divine love and return to our point of origin. Put differently, the natural environment of *Homo Sapiens* is heaven, and we cannot truly flourish in any less wholesome context. Even our more dark and midnight desires are just noisome and misdirected expressions of a more basic desire to be at one with God. For example, gratified lust counterfeits God's creativity and power sought for its own sake parodies God's omnipotence. The land of unlikeness is unreal because it denies the essential wholesomeness of human nature.

Occasionally, I go to the Denver Museum of Natural History to watch the stuffed animals in their glass cases. I have been doing this since I was in grade school. Years ago the curators posed a herd of stuffed deer in one of the cases against a painting of mountains and streams. Then they surrounded the deer with aspen logs, wax leaves, and other faux tokens of the wilderness. The whole effect is fairly realistic and rather beautiful. The stuffed deer seem much like real deer, and even the stuffed chipmunk clinging to the dead aspen bark is lifelike. Yet the scene is beautiful because it mimics life, not because it is itself alive. The deer will never grow, flourish, or be replaced by their stuffed fawns. The chipmunk will never complete his dash around the tree trunk. Rather, the display I saw as a boy will be just the same if I go to visit it this afternoon, next month, or next year.

Similarly, the land of unlikeness is at best a static place that mimics actual living. The things we see there might be interesting or, in their derivative way, beautiful, but they can never compare with communion with God himself. One may encounter good and beautiful things in the land of unlikeness, but such things are good and beautiful only insofar as they imitate the goodness or beauty of the real order established and loved by God. The land of unlikeness is to our authentic existence as a shadow is to the object which casts it.

Group Projects

The land of unlikeness may be either an individual effort or a group project, but since the group projects are usually easier to discern, let us begin there. No doubt most of us have had the experience of living or working with a pathological organization and of making one's own contribution to the group's unhappiness. Several years ago I was asked to teach a couple of courses at a college more than an hour's drive from my home. The department I taught in had organized itself around a charismatic and hard-driving department chair. This fellow was extremely good at getting funding and generally advancing the cause of his department chiefly because he was not reticent about, and probably enjoyed, bullying anyone who got in his way. Apparently, faculty members thought that the results he obtained more than compensated for his disposition.

Since I only taught one evening a week, I was able to observe the professors from a distance as they coped with the results of their choice of leaders. The first thing I noticed was that these people were always on edge. The department chair was always on guard against threats both outside and inside the department, and, from time to time, spat a stream of venom at one or another of his underlings. I noticed that these people spent a great deal of time milling around in the halls talking departmental and university politics. Conversations almost always turned to who was enraged by what and by whom.

Worse, it seemed that the faculty feared one another. Since each of them was a potential favorite or target of the chairman's anger, there was a constant, though very polite, jockeying for position. Everyone always wanted to appear in the best light possible. I suppose this was a way of making oneself safe. At the same time, they wanted to appear as though they were a happy family. The department chair was known to give bottles of wine to subordinates he had badgered the previous day, and at Christmas time everyone exchanged nice gifts.

Needless to say, I had had enough of the place after a semester, and decided to stay closer to home. But I did learn something about myself. If I had not been so much of an outsider, I would not have been so aware of that department's oddness and would probably have been sucked right into the game. People choose academic careers, particularly in the humanities, because they love the subject matter and welcome the opportunity to teach. Consequently, they are willing to sacrifice and accommodate in order to get on with their work. Rightly directed, this can foster a mild and generous temperament. However, a spirit of appeasement and compromise can foster collusion with overweening power and failure to recognize and oppose cruelty. Had I been a full-time faculty member in that department, I doubt that I could have done better.

Individual Narrowness

I am quite capable of visiting the land of unlikeness without leaving home. A central theme in my life has been a largely unsuccessful search for security and stability, and some of my worst behavior stems from this perceived need. For instance, if I feel sufficiently set on edge by external circumstances, I promptly notice clutter around the house or the dirty dishes in the sink. Being a fairly fastidious person myself and since only two of us live here, I immediately roust Barbara and dun her for not cleaning up after herself. While I may have a point, I tend to invest it with more gravity than a matter of mere housekeeping merits. Unless I come to myself, I will wind up hurting her feelings.

A sense of stability and security is important for me because when I was in my mid-teens my family had to sell our farm and move to the suburbs. Our world literally shrank, and it felt like it kept shrinking. Rather than living in a nineteenth century farm house surrounded by fields and orchards, we found ourselves in a tract house surrounded by unnaturally green lawns and car ports. I sought a sense of control where I could find it: in my studies and by keeping my surroundings very much in order. In fact, I came to associate disorder with decay and diminution, and so untidiness still tends to unnerve me. Then I married someone with no such inhibitions about housekeeping and began learning to set aside that crutch. So far, my results have been, at best, middling, but Barbara and I expect to have the matter sorted-out in a couple of decades.

I mention these individual and corporate examples not to elicit smugness or pity but to illustrate that the land of unlikeness frequently traffics in fear and perceived neediness. No doubt, each of us could supply many more such examples. Fortunately, God's love can draw us clear of irrational fear and self-imposed neediness and into new, wide-open territory. As Saint John liked to say, God is greater than the human heart (see 1 John 3.20). These wide-open spaces of the spirit, like the pearl of great price (see Matthew 13.45–46) are something for which one would gladly trade anything else. Christian liberty means having permission to pursue wonder and delight without counting costs. To say exactly the same thing in different words, Christian liberty means possessing the freedom to live with integrity.

Grace and the Return to the Divine Likeness

Oftentimes in the Bible we see a swift and decisive response to God's grace. For instance, the first disciples immediately left their nets to follow Christ (see Mark 1.16–20), and Saint Paul promptly began preaching the gospel after his experience on the road to Damascus (see Acts 9.1–22). Yet most of us require a lengthy period after our conversion in which to become accustomed to sensing God's presence and seeing the world in the way God sees it. During this period, the basic facets of the experience of conversion are intensified and its fruits become part of our own moral and psychological equipment. In conversion we sense that we have come from God and will return to God, and by embarking on the purgative way we begin working out the pragmatic features of our return.

Traditionally, Christian mystics compare the first steps on the way back to God to the ancient Israelites' wanderings in the desert. In the Old Testament the wilderness was both a fearsome place and a place where God's activity was particularly evident. In the wilderness God formed the Israelites into the chosen people, and the chosen people learned to anticipate a land of milk and honey rather than look backward toward their slavery in Egypt. God used the desert in the way a surgeon uses a scalpel to remove a tumor. Just as a sharp knife can divide healthy and malignant flesh, the clarity of the wilderness separated what was essential and inessential to Israel's relationship with God.

Similarly, Christian mystics have always sought out the solitude of the wilderness. In the desert the peripheral features of the mystic's life fall away. Distractions are unavailable and pretense futile. Ambitions, lusts, and grudges are revealed for what they are, and God reveals himself as he is. In its initial phases, the life of the desert consists in a series of banal or embarrassing confrontations with oneself, but one may also expect an increasingly intimate awareness of God's presence. The desert is the setting for both remediation and adventure. One finds both the plodding work of acquiring true simplicity and the thrill of discovering a horizon that extends further than one had imagined.

Antony and the Demons

In the case of Antony of Egypt (250?–356) we find a literal journey into the wilderness. Having distributed his possessions among the friends and neighbors, Antony made his way to the old pagan tombs on the outskirts of his village. There, the legends say, Antony encountered demons who assumed the crocodilian and birdlike forms of the old gods. They beat him into unconsciousness. It is fitting that Antony is said to have begun his career as a monk struggling with the false gods of his hometown. A god, after all, is anything that promises to give our lives ultimate meaning. The first idols many of us encounter are the dusty household divinities of respectability, propriety, and circumspection. We worry about how others will see us and develop false fronts calculated to please. Worse, we eventually mistake these facades for our true natures.

I have sometimes listened to shopkeepers speaking reverently about the free market and football coaches praising the nuclear family. There always seemed to be a note of strident desperation in their words, as if the passion with which they said something could get them affluence or respectability. There are many false gods: tradition, the respect of one's peers, right religion, the outward appearance of success, etc. But things of this kind are only substitutes for God himself.

The first commandment of the wilderness is: "I am the LORD your God, who brought you out of the land of Egypt, out of the house of slavery, you will have no other gods before me" (Exodus 20.1). The corresponding first temptation is to idolatry. In the wilderness idolatry begins as a nostalgia which confuses creation with the Creator and assumes that some remembered, subsidiary good can take the place of God. Subsidiary goods become idols when we fail to recognize them as gifts of divine providence. One's pre-conversion mentality reasserts itself, and one pines for the old dispensation. What was once abandoned as an encumbrance is sought again as a guarantee of security. Yet the old crutches no longer help; they only bring pain. To return to Aelred's allegory, the land of unlikeness is as it is because those dwelling in it grasp at gods instead of seeking God himself.

The first order of business in the desert is the stripping away of outward pretense so that the divine likeness might be revealed. The first lesson is that God will not tolerate phonies, and the first precept is unflinching honesty. God demands that we stand before him as we really are, no more and no less. Such honesty is frightening and, oftentimes, painful. Yet it is also liberating and even exhilarating. One begins to sense a solidity in oneself as a child of God created in the divine image and likeness. The essence of Antony's first encounter with the demons consists in the temptation to continue wearing a mask, and to continue worshiping the gods of stability, respectability, and inoffensiveness. Antony declines, and although he comes away from the struggle bruised, he walks away free.

Thoreau and the Desperate Debtors

Henry David Thoreau (1817–1862) loved the woods, he said, because there one had time to be more than a machine. Thoreau was a Massachusetts Yankee, and the false god he set out to unmask was the Protestant work ethic. All around him Thoreau saw people throwing themselves into commercial activity with the dour intensity of Indian fakirs taking to their beds of nails. Yet while the latter form of self-torture would have been frowned upon even in Concord, Massachusetts's most forward-thinking circles, the former was a matter of civic pride. Six days a week, the hardworking citizens of Concord rose early to labor for long hours at tasks they clearly did not enjoy.

Seeking an explanation of this phenomenon, Thoreau made discreet inquiries at the Concord courthouse and discovered that only a handful of his friends and neighbors owned their property free and clear. The majority lived as anxious debtors beholden to their creditors. They worked to service their debts, and so the civic virtue of being steadily employed was the virtue of a servant, not that of a free person. Thoreau had this respectable, middle-class debt peonage in mind when he penned the famous sentence, "The mass of men lead lives of quiet desperation."[1] Consumed by work, Thoreau's friends and neighbors could afford neither the time nor energy to tend to those matters which make a life worth living.

Thoreau recognized that such beetling debt was unnecessary and that a full life could be lived at little expense. To prove his point, and to enjoy himself while doing so, he built a small cabin near Walden Pond and moved into it on July 4th, 1845, Independence Day. Yet Thoreau was no whimsical dabbler at self-sufficiency. The early pages of *Walden* contain detailed budgets and thorough plans for growing food, procuring shelter, and staying warm in winter. Thoreau was also a tradesman. Well versed in carpentry and surveying, Thoreau traded his skills to procure what he could not produce for himself. By keeping to a simple life, Thoreau enjoyed both a richer life *and* a greater net worth than many of the outwardly prosperous but heavily indebted citizens of Concord.

One of the chief lessons we can learn from Thoreau is that in the wilderness credit cards are useless except, perhaps, for fuel. As a longtime student and sometime college instructor I have often been saddened seeing students accrue large credit card and student loan debts and then at graduation resign themselves to living in the "real world"— as if debt peonage were more substantial than learning about oneself and the nature of the world. Sometimes in my classes a civic-minded student will tell me that religion is important because it helps preserve order in society. I usually reply that easy credit has been far more effective.

---

1. Henry David Thoreau, *Walden; or, Life in the Woods* (1854; Mineola, NY: Dover Publications, 1995), 4.

Nonetheless, one might object that what Thoreau says is of little value now because self-sufficiency is no longer a viable option for most people and because he has nothing to say about raising a family.

If the first objection is correct, and it really is impossible for most people to live without servicing a debt, then we will simply have to admit that the United States is no longer home to large numbers of people who enjoy positive economic freedom. At the very least, this places a greater responsibility for doing so upon those of us who can. The second objection often implies that one must be prosperous in order to raise happy children. This is false. While I have met many young people who resented their parents for neglecting them for the sake of their jobs, I have never met a child who resented his or her parents because of their poverty. The journey back to God may well require leading a life of honorable simplicity. But such simplicity like that of the lilies of the field (see Matthew 6.26–29) gives us permission to shine as the creatures God made us to be.

Christ in the Desert

Saint Matthew's gospel tells us that the Holy Spirit led Jesus into the wilderness where he was tempted by the devil (Matthew 4.1–11; see also Luke 4.1–13). The devil approaches Jesus with three propositions, inviting him to turn stones to bread, to hurl himself from the pinnacle of the temple, and to place personal power ahead of doing the Father's will. The first two temptations traffic in wants and fears, and are intended to foster dawdling and complacency on the journey. The third seeks directly to undermine Jesus's reasons for being in the desert at all by redirecting his search for the Father's will into a self-aggrandizing quest for control of his circumstances.

Jesus is worn down from fasting, and so the devil first probes his anxiety about his physical well-being. "If you are the son of God," says the devil, "command these stones to become loaves of bread" (Matthew 4.3). Here the devil assumes that if Jesus could turn the stones to bread, then he would do so, thereby both proving his status as son of God and allaying the fear which accompanies intense hunger. As we have already seen, those in loving relationships do not desire proofs, and a loving relationship with God draws us beyond our limited knowledge of ourselves and of God. Jesus' response, then, is to be expected: "One does not live by bread alone, but by every word that comes from the mouth of God" (Matthew 4.4). In effect, Jesus tells the devil that the richness of the desert journey would go unnoticed were he to become obsessed with satisfying physical needs. The adventure would degenerate into wool gathering or, worse, gainful employment.

Then the probing becomes more astute. The devil spirits Jesus away to Jerusalem and sets him on the pinnacle of the temple. "If you are the Son of God," says the devil, "throw yourself down for it is written, 'He will command his angels concerning you,' and 'On their hands they will bear you up, so that you will not dash your foot against a stone' " (Matthew 4.6). Here the temptation is not downward into excessive concern over one's physical well-being but upward into a giddy religiosity. It is the temptation to bask in uncreated light like a well-fed tabby cat rather than honestly to confront the difficulties facing one.

In the devil-inspired vision Jesus finds himself in a precarious position, and one way out is through an expedient miracle. Jesus replies, "Again it is written, 'Do not put the

Lord your God to the test' " (Matthew 4.7). When we find ourselves perched against our will on the dizzying pinnacle of the temple, the proper response is to get to work climbing down. Just as it is a mistake to become obsessed with physical or financial security, it is also improper to use religion to flee challenges life sets before us. If the former is an error of timidity, the latter is one of braggadocio.

In an ancient legend of the desert, a young man named John decided that he would enjoy being an angel ceaselessly worshiping God. Immediately, he threw off his cloak and wandered out into the Egyptian wilderness. In a few days he was back at his brother's door asking to be fed. The brother replied that the man on the doorstep could not be John since he had become an angel. When John insisted that it was he, the brother opened the door saying that since John was a human being once again he would have work in order to eat. The point of the story is not that we all ought to be hard at work but that religious faith should never be used to escape from one's life and responsibilities.

The third temptation is not designed to probe fears but to elicit despair. Again the devil spirits Jesus away, this time to a high mountain, shows him all the kingdoms of the earth, and says, "All these will I give you, if you fall down and worship me" (Matthew 4.9). Now the devil directly attacks Jesus's status as a child of God, offering Jesus a derivative cosmic lordship as his underling. The temptation is to despair of God's loving presence and to console oneself through the acquisition and exercise of power. Rather than trusting in God, Jesus is tempted to run things for himself. Jesus responds by reiterating the cardinal principle of the desert: "It is written, 'Worship the Lord your God and serve only him' " (Matthew 4.10).

The Work of the Wilderness

To the biblical mind the wilderness is a holy place in which one may enter into communion with God. It is a place where one can clearly sense God's sustenance, and, more importantly, it is a place where one learns to turn habitually toward God. We may arrive in the desert by different paths. We may, like Antony, journey there of our own accord, or we may, like Jesus or Elijah (see 1 Kings 19.4–9) be led there by the hidden work of the Holy Spirit. Once we arrive, however, the geography is the same. The clear and penetrating light of the desert requires that we remove the layers of fear and pretense we thought we needed in the land of unlikeness and recognize these as the unnecessary baggage they are. Now is the time for honesty. The desert demands that we discover who we really are and that we persevere in this knowledge. There is, in short, only one rule for the desert pilgrim: God created you in his image, seek his likeness.

I have already alluded to two paths into the wilderness, namely, the way one actively chooses and the way one accepts as a gift from God. Both are salutary insofar as both originate in love and aim at divine union. In the traditional terminology, these two paths are referred to, respectively, as active and passive purgation. By entering into the way of active purgation one seeks to replicate one or more of the conditions of the desert in order to be attentive to God's presence. In passive purgation it is God who takes the lead. Generally speaking, this second class of purgations tends to be both more intimate and more efficacious. I will discuss passive purgation in detail in the next chapter. However, let us turn first to active purgation.

The purpose of active purgation is to recover the divine likeness by developing a habitual, loving awareness of God. When properly practiced, active purgation will always focus on the goal of divine union rather than on the methods one deploys to achieve it. One of the classic spiritual errors is to mistake one's techniques for the end one seeks to achieve by those techniques. For example, I would be deluded if I thought that I was on the right track *because* I was up at 6:00 a.m. Sunday morning to attend the earliest Holy Communion service. Rather, getting up at 6:00 a.m. *might* contribute to a habitual awareness of God's presence *provided that* I keep the point of the exercise in mind. For these reasons, it is usually best to discuss what one is doing with a clear-headed friend. If we are lucky, God blesses us with people who both love us and refuse to take us overly seriously, and it is never wise to refuse God's gifts.

The traditional ascetical tools include: solitude, fasting, and vigils. This much is worth emphasizing: these are traditional practices which some have found helpful in seeking and being found by God. In themselves, they are neither good nor bad and certainly not, in themselves, indicative of holiness. It is futile to think of them as ways of collecting merit badges from the divine scoutmaster. Since past generations have found solitude, fasting and vigils helpful, these practices may offer us a good starting point.

Solitude

Solitude is one of the defining features of the wilderness. When one is alone with God two distinct opportunities emerge. In the first place, one can be more attentive to the work of the Holy Spirit inside when freed a while from competing, outside concerns. Oftentimes, God chooses to be subtle, and his subtle activity can go unnoticed if one's world is full of jabbering televisions or idle chatter. In solitude one comes to know God as an engaging, and often witty, companion on the day's journey rather than as an occasionally-glimpsed, stern presence. In this way, solitude often has a unique sweetness and beauty.

Solitude also provides an arena for confrontations with oneself. Without other people or household appliances creating distractions, the mind is thrown back on itself, and one's interior dialogue or stream of consciousness assumes a new prominence. Old resentments and fresh lusts bubble to the top of one's consciousness together with regret and ambition. While spending a day alone, one might imagine being elected to city council and running a town from behind a big mahogany desk, before noticing that the image of the desk is more pleasing than the paperwork on top of it. Similarly, one might fantasize about becoming the beloved author of spiritual classics only to recognize more of a taste for notoriety than a desire to be helpful.

As one passes through the wilderness on the way back to God, one discovers a new depth and efficaciousness at prayer. Previously one might have thought that prayer consisted in saying things to God and that it trafficked only in words and mental images. In the desert the words and images fall away, and one is left with a simple awareness of God's presence. The subtle presence of God is as palpable as that of a friend or lover, and yet one does not see God. Rather, it is as though for a moment in the corner of one's eye one glimpses God passing. No words or images can do justice to this awareness, for it is of God himself no longer cloaked by his creation. One feels caught up in God's presence and transformed by it. The experience does not seem odd or wholly different from what has gone before. It is as one thought it might be.

Those intent on seeking and being found by God have always felt drawn to solitude. Some withdraw to remote places or the silence of monasteries and convents. Yet the essential features of the wilderness are always found within us, wherever we may find ourselves. Once one has determined to set aside pretense and to strive to see God as he is, one has entered the desert. Now I am not suggesting that, say, the floor of the Chicago Board of Trade is as felicitous a place to meet God as a remote grove of aspen trees. Rather, with the right disposition one could meet God at the Chicago Board of Trade, and without it one will miss God even in the aspen grove.

Desert dwellers in Saint Antony's day used to tell newcomers, "Stay in your cell, and your cell will teach you everything." Similarly, someone interested in experiencing God in solitude need only find an out of the way place, go there for a few hours, and pay attention. Perhaps one will have to wait a bit for God to show himself, but this is unimportant because one is in the divine presence already. At such times one might read a few pages of the Bible, examine one's conscience, or simply admire the blue of the sky. These sorts of things are all profitably done while waiting, but they should not be allowed to interfere with attentiveness to God himself, the reason one entered into solitude in the first place. Moreover, it is probably not a good idea for a solitary to perform various devotions as a way of cajoling God into manifesting himself. This sort of behavior strikes me as analogous to that of a child who grabs a magician by the lapels and demands that he perform his tricks. Rather, as John Milton says in one of his sonnets:

> God doth not need
> Either man's work or his own gifts. Who best
> Bear his mild yoke, they serve him best. His state
> Is kingly: thousands at his bidding speed,
> And post o'er land and ocean without rest;
> They also serve who only stand and wait.

The defining feature of the proficient solitary is loving attentiveness. Standing and waiting is itself service. The rest is God's concern.

Fasting

When I was a graduate student I used to skip meals. When I skipped lunch I was not so sleepy in the afternoon. My mind had a sharper edge to it, and I could study better. I rarely bought meat. It was expensive, and I could use the extra money to buy books. I was not unique. My friends also discovered that they could keep their minds clear by skipping meals and subsisted on ramen noodles. One of my friends used to pay for a large coffee, fill the cup half way, and top it off with free half-and-half. The menu at graduate student dinner parties often consisted of spaghetti and a bottle of the cheapest chianti we could find. My friends and I would not have thought of this as fasting. We would have said that we were pursuing our educations.

We were fasting, of course. To fast is to abstain from food or to eat only simple food for the sake of some other good. We wanted to learn things, and the ramen noodles and milky coffee served that end. Sometimes when people feel lethargic or sleepy when they are trying to pray a bit of fasting will help. One will probably feel somewhat less tired and more clear-headed. However, we all have to eat. Eventually one has to learn to study on a full stomach and to pray when feeling tired or sluggish.

Fasting is something easily overdone. Our bodies are designed for regular feedings, and to ignore this fact on a regular basis invites trouble. Stomach problems are a common problem for graduate students. The problems do not come from stress so much as from self-abuse. After becoming acquainted, new Ph.D.'s often exchange stories about skipping meals and then trade advice about prescription medicines for stomach problems. So fast if you must, but avoid it when you can.

Gardening

A better way accomplish the purpose of a fast is to plant a garden. An old farmer once told me that a well-tended plot of ground is good for a person physically, morally, and financially. I tend to agree with him. In addition to being good exercise, digging and weeding provides an opportunity to practice self-discipline. For example, if I can finish hoeing a row of corn when I am hot and sweaty, I will have that much more will power to bring to bear on other, more important, projects. Manual labor brings a wholesome tiredness and, oftentimes, a special stillness at prayer. One's body may ache a bit, but one can also enjoy a sense of having cooperated with the Creator in keeping the world fertile and well-ordered. Gardens are also beautiful places, and one can honor the Creator simply by appreciating the beauty of a time of day or a season there.

Additionally, by growing some of one's own food more resources become available to help those who cannot.

Resources which I do not use could be of much more importance to someone else, and my garden creates the possibility. Gardeners can extend their reach even further by donating the money they save on food to charities which promote agricultural self-sufficiency in the Third World. Granted, a single backyard vegetable garden will have an almost nugatory effect on world hunger. However, it offers the individual an immediate and tangible way of making a difference, and I think it would be a mistake to underestimate the effect of a hundred or a thousand such gardens.

One of my friends is an avid gardener. Once she told me about a woman came to her parish to get a few staples from the church's food bank. My friend happened to be the only person around and had no keys to the church basement where the food was kept. Instead, she did what one is never supposed to do: she invited the woman to her house and scoured her pantry for spaghetti and a couple jars of her home-made sauce. Then she took the woman out to the garden and the two picked some peas and lettuce. Often people who come to a food bank seem embarrassed or ashamed to ask for a few cans of vegetables or a bag of rice. Yet out in the garden my friend claims there was less of this unease. Perhaps it was just the inadvertent personal touch, but I also like to think that it had something to do with the garden itself. In a garden, earth, water, and sunlight become food in a nearly gratuitous manner, and my friend had the opportunity not so much to do a favor as share a blessing.

Keeping Vigils

To return to our discussion of traditional ascetical practices, another of the standard tools of the desert is the vigil. Keeping a vigil consists in changing one's pattern of sleeping and using tiredness or the stillness of the night to foster a quiet attentiveness to God's presence. Traditionally, a vigil involves rising either in the middle of the night or before dawn to meditate on the scriptures or simply to wait for God to give a sign of his presence. In either case, the key to the vigil is attention.

The Christian tradition recommends vigils to those who are discouraged or in danger of giving up on the journey back to God. Discouragement, of course, originates in a loss of hope. One doubts that he or she will arrive at the place set out for and so no longer looks forward to getting there. This is one of the great dangers of the desert. Without faith and hope love is impossible, and without love God is unable to dwell within us. For this reason, many of the earliest Christian texts emphasize staying awake and waiting for the Master's return (e.g., Matthew 25.1–13; Luke 12.35–38; 1 Thessalonians 5.6–8). A vigil is an exercise in hope. Simply doing it is an act of faith, and where there is faith love and hope are also present. By waiting one hopes, and in hoping one loves.

Recently, I discovered a new way of keeping a vigil. Sometimes before dawn I drive up Lookout Mountain and sit with my back to a cold rock to watch the sun rise over Denver. At first, I sit in the dark watching a lake of lights shimmer all the way out to the horizon. Then a thin line of blue sky appears in the east, and a half-dozen magpies sail over me and then down the hill. Sometimes I notice a herd of deer grazing below me in the half-light. The sun abruptly breaks over the horizon. The deer pause a moment and look back toward it sensing the first touch of its warmth, and I notice that my hand casts a shadow. I am substantial again and ready to return home for a bowl of cereal and a cup of coffee.

Chapter 3

False Summits

Since Love will thrust in itself as the greatest of all principles, let us at last willingly allow it room. . . . It seems it will break in everywhere, as that without which the world could not be enjoyed.

—Thomas Traherne, *Centuries*, IV.61

How God Saves Us from "God"

At least once each summer I like to climb Byers Peak, a 12,804-foot mountain near Frasier, Colorado. The hike is not difficult, and from the top there is a fine view of the Continental Divide and of a valley with a river winding through it. Often from the summit I have watched mountain goats skipping across the boulder fields below me. Since I am familiar with the mountain's topography, I can estimate how long the ascent will take and what work awaits me at different points along the trail. The first time a friend and I climbed the mountain this was not so. Having sweated through the spruce forest and krummholz and reached timberline, we found a steep upward path edged by alpine flowers. We set ourselves upon it. The trail wound upward toward a granite promontory, and my friend and I congratulated ourselves for reaching the top of the peak in good time.

Yet as we approached the granite knob, we groaned as the true summit of Byers Peak rose behind it. Eventually we reached the top, but the hike was more difficult than we had at first supposed.

Something similar occurs in the desert as God begins to present himself to us as he actually is. As we begin to sense God's immediate, intimate presence our preconceptions about him begin to drop away, and those things which once appeared as pinnacles of spiritual awareness are now revealed as mere resting places on the journey to God himself. In the wilderness our preconceptions about God and what it is to be a holy person are regularly revealed to be false summits when we glimpse the true nature of God rising up behind our notions of how God ought to be. As Meister Eckhart (1260–1329) used to say, God in his mercy can free us even from our own concept of "God."

God Takes the Lead

Having glimpsed God in desert solitude, one is disabused of trite notions of piety and personal holiness. The scripts by which one has run his or her life drop away, and one's stock of Sunday school certainties and grade school truisms are revealed as banalities. One finds oneself in unmapped territory, and it will be difficult to gauge what counts as success or failure by the old standards. Instead, it is best simply to be faithful to the experience and to continue in the hope that through it one will come to love God and all creation more.

Although one may not perceive it, this is a crucial moment since now it is God who takes the initiative. Rather than seeking grace one is now led by it, and sometimes it seems as though God himself is designing unique purgations. Western mystics often refer to this aspect of the soul's development as "passive purgation," because God rather than the individual takes the active role in the journey out of the land of unlikeness. One simply has to remain receptive to God's work. Passive purgation is an especially important manifestation of the Holy Spirit because in it God can be seen drawing a person beyond the narrow bounds of his or her particular life and into the light and expansiveness of divine communion.

Often initial reactions to God's activity range from anger to vertigo to mourning. This much is to be expected. I suspect we have an instinct for psychic self-preservation, and an overturning of cherished conceptions about God and oneself is likely to be experienced as a threat to one's well being. Our instincts tell us to retrench or to hide from what God has begun in us, but the real danger at this point is a failure of nerve. One is tempted back toward the familiar. One may even try forcing God to be as we would like rather than to let him be as he is. Put in the language of the New Testament, such a failure of nerve is tantamount to the temptation to live by bread rather than by God's word (see Matthew 4.3–4).

Garlic and Cucumbers

Wandering in the wilderness the children of Israel frequently allowed fear and nostalgia to trump faith. While being led into the land of milk and honey and feeding on bread from heaven, they looked back wistfully to slavery in Egypt:

> If only we had meat to eat! We remember the fish we used to eat in Egypt for nothing, the cucumbers, the melons, the

leeks, the onions, and the garlic; but now our strength is dried up, and there is nothing at all but this manna to look at. (Numbers 11.4–6)

Jesus once asked, "What will it profit them to gain the whole world and forfeit their life?" (Mark 8.36). But for a cucumber? Unfortunately, when God sends one such an opportunity it is all too easy to make an equally absurd deal or forget that God is in control of the experience.

Last summer Barbara and I visited the Denver Botanical Gardens. We wandered among the different plantings until we came to the herb beds. There among garlic and basil was a clump of Egyptian onions. The Egyptian onion is an ancient variety which sets its bulbs on the top of its stems. I had been looking for such a plant for several years. When I saw these, I made sure that no one was looking, pulled a couple of bulbs off one of the stems, and slipped them into my pocket. It was a perfect and virtually victimless crime. When Barbara and I got to the parking lot, however, I found that someone had broken into my car and stolen the stereo. Passive purgation works something like this.

Shortly after defending my dissertation on Aristotle's *De Anima* I found myself leading morning prayer at my parish. It was the feast of Saint Clement of Alexandria (150–220), one of the first Christians to examine the faith in light of Greek philosophy. It was a weekday morning, and only a handful of us were there. I was pleased with myself since I could now be called "Dr. Simpson" and smugly delighted to be celebrating the feast of a colleague. The smugness lasted until I read the collect of the day from *Lesser Feasts and Fasts*:

O Lord, you called your servant Clement of Alexandria from the errors of ancient philosophy that he might learn and teach the saving Gospel of Christ: Turn your Church from the conceits of worldly wisdom and, by the spirit of truth, guide it into all truth; through Jesus Christ our Lord, who lives and reigns with you and the Holy Spirit, one God, for ever and ever. Amen.

I stopped halfway through the collect laughing, and everyone laughed with or at me. Sometimes these things happen.

Almost all experiences of passive purgation have a bit of comedy in them. The joke usually turns on the seeker discovering more than had been sought. One searches for what one expects God to be like, but one finds God himself. Often it seems as though God takes particular delight in flouting these expectations. According to legend, the fourteenth-century German mystic Meister Eckhart encountered a handsome, naked boy while walking in the forest. When Eckhart asked the boy where he came from and where he was going, the boy responded, "I came from God and I am returning to God." When Eckhart asked him who he was, the boy responded, "a king." Eckhart led the boy-king to his cell and offered to let him take whatever coat he wanted. The boy responded, "Then I would no longer be a king," and then vanished. It was God himself who, we are told, was having a bit of fun.

(1) Clinging to What We Think God Might Be

Passive purgation aims at getting us free from three kinds of misconceptions. On the journey back to the divine likeness, one may cling to what one already possesses, grasp at what one does not possess, or throw aside the good one has or the hope of at last possessing it. God wills none of this. Rather, the point of passive purgation is to allow us to give up clinging and grasping, insofar as this keeps us from God, and to keep us from giving up hope while the cure is in progress. It gives me no pleasure to write about clinging, grasping, and despair. Nonetheless, one often runs across them in the desert, and, as scoutmasters tell us, forewarned is forearmed. God willing, someday we will look back at these false summits and laugh. Let us begin by looking at several ways people cling to what they have.

Pastors often encounter parishioners who can tell them many correct things about God. These people are quite ready to affirm that Christ died for our sins, that the Trinity consists of three persons but one nature, that human beings were made in the image and likeness of God, or that love is the greatest of the theological virtues. Yet they behave as if they had spent the last couple of hours sitting on a cake of ice. They seem not to perceive the engaging puzzle of the Trinity's plural singularity or take to heart the potential for union with the divine through love. Rather, they are satisfied, and cock their snoots at people of dubious orthodoxy or mutter that some people are not firm enough on the Bible, the classical heresies, or sin generally. My clergy friends tell me that these people are often the most unhappy and impervious in a parish.

The problem here is not excessive orthodoxy but a failure to take to heart the true scope of Christian liberty. Lived Christianity is not so much a matter of holding correct opinions about the divinity but of drawing close to God and being taken up in God's loving vision of the world. God became a man so that we might become one with God. The slippage begins as soon as we mistake what orthodox belief says about God for God himself and take up loving some notion of God rather than God himself. Confusing a notion of God with God himself is a mistake about categories and is similar to what happens when one confuses a map with the territory the map represents.

When I was in grade school, our teachers used to hang big maps of the world on our classroom walls. From the idle time I spent looking at these maps, I somehow got the impression that Greenland was larger than Australia. The reason was that the maps were all Mercator projections. In order to represent the round earth on a flat, unbroken surface, the map makers had to distort the size of land masses near the poles. This is what made Greenland look so large in relation to Australia. In order to be complete, the maps had to be distorted. Similarly, Christian orthodoxy is an attempt to flatten God out by representing him by means of the words and images of our three dimensions and five senses. Yet by its very nature Christian orthodoxy has more to say about how humanity experiences God than about God himself. After all, God already knows himself through and through, and so the Christian revelation and Christian theology is not for his benefit but for ours. This is not so say that Christian orthodoxy is a failure, only that it is a limited success achieved with limited resources.

Alone in the Sandwich Boards

A few years ago, I watched a street preacher haranguing people outside the student union at the University of

Colorado at Boulder. The preacher wore a sandwich board. One panel bore a message that any Christian could agree with, namely, that God loves humanity and that Christ died for sinners. The other panel listed who counted as a sinner, and this pretty much included anyone who disagreed with the preacher's reading of the Bible. The second panel did not set quite the right tone. Some of the students began pelting him with idle questions about dinosaurs or about how God will manage to resurrect the bodies of missionaries who get themselves eaten by cannibals. When someone asked the preacher how he could be so sure his audience was bound for hell, he hissed, "Because you're scoffers."

Then the preacher began singing. One of the lines of his tune was, "The B-I-B-L-E that is the book for me." I was embarrassed because the Bible is my book too. I watched with a certain amount of sadness and boredom as the preacher invoked the Bible to validate his cramped and cranky view of the world. Then somebody yelled for him to sing "Amazing Grace," and something remarkable happened. Alone inside his sandwich boards, the man sang of divine and gratuitous love. The words and melody forced him simply to stand for a moment in God's presence as a pilgrim. I cannot say for sure what happened in that moment, but it seemed as though in that instant he had attained both genuine humility and real dignity. In that moment he was saved, seeing, and found, and even some of his tormentors sang with him. I had hoped that he would read from the Beatitudes or, perhaps, from one of the letters of Saint John the Divine. Instead, the preacher returned to his rant. The desultory bickering started up again, and he was able to save no souls that afternoon.

Institutions and the Body of Christ

Passive purgation often involves God drawing us beyond the map orthodoxy provides and into the fresh, open territory of greater love. A similar sort of confusion occurs when one mistakes the mystical body of Christ for one or another of the institutions which might clothe it. In this instance, it is not that God himself gets mistaken for orthodoxy's map of him but, rather, the marvelous fusion of the human and the divine gets mistaken for one or another of its social or historical manifestations. For example, some of my Roman Catholic friends mourn the disappearance of thriving convents, monasteries, and seminaries. They take this as evidence that their Church is imperiled or, perhaps, dying. Some react by attempting to close ranks and call for greater obedience to authority or a self-conscious return to the practices of earlier generations.

I am not sure that Roman Catholic institutions really are rolling up everywhere in the world. Yet even if this were the case, I would not think this counts as evidence that the Body of Christ is being irreparably damaged. On the contrary, I suspect that God is just as active now as he ever was, and that he will continue to draw people to him however he sees fit. This may or may not involve the institutions of the Roman Catholic Church, and it may or may not involve the institutions of my own Episcopal Church. Fortunately, it is not necessary that the power of God's love and Christian fellowship be bottled up in any one organization. This simple fact should be of some consolation in an era when many religious institutions appear to be atrophying. Rather than clinging to the past, perhaps it is best to give a decent burial to any institutions which no longer help God show himself to those who seek him.

(2) Grasping at What One Does Not Possess

In addition to clinging to what one possesses, one journeying back to God may want to hurry grace and grasp at what he or she has not yet attained. When this happens, the uniqueness and authenticity of the desert journey is in danger. Rather than glimpsing the God of the wilderness as he is, one tries to work up a notion of what God might be like in order to have an experience of *that*—whatever *that* may be. In doing this, one becomes both the arbitrator and initiator of the experience while God is left to cool his heels somewhere outside the frame of the well-thought-out picture.

The ancient authors of the psalms were well aware that the desire for a God made in our image is both idolatrous and ripe for satire. An anonymous poet imagined a peeved and sardonic divinity looking in on the elaborate rituals of the Jerusalem temple:

> If I were hungry, I would not tell you,
> for the world and all that is in it is mine.
> Do I eat the flesh of bulls or drink the blood of goats?
> (Psalm 50.12–13)

The psalmist's point is a simple one. God wishes to reveal himself to us, and the best thing we can do is be receptive and grateful for that revelation. Without this basic attitude, any of our attempts to establish relations with God will be empty, futile, and ultimately comical. As the psalmist puts it, "Those who bring thanksgiving as their sacrifice honor me" (Psalm 50.22). It seems quaint to us that ancient people could imagine God patting his stomach after a sturdy meal of beef and goat's blood. Yet we have our own stock of seedy anthropomorphisms. I would suggest, for example, that current wrangles about the gender of the divinity have about the same level of theological sophistication as that of the ancient goats' blood theorists.

As we progress further into the wilderness, it becomes increasingly important to allow one's experience of God to be *one's own* experience. The essence of the desert journey consists in a personal encounter with God's redemptive power, and if I am faithful to it, I will become more and more myself. The facades and pretenses will fall away, and finally I will be left to stand in God's loving presence as I truly am. It is imperative that one's encounter with God not be pre-scripted by oneself or pre-chewed by others. Rather than grasping at what I do not have, it is vitally important that I dispose myself to receive it as a gift from God and wait patiently to receive it.

One of the more dismal aberrations I encountered in the study of religious anthropology was the phenomenon of cargo cults. A typical cargo cult develops when a tribal culture encounters a superior technology, and the symbols of that technology supplant indigenous religious practices. Matches, transistor radios, and other "cargo" get interpreted as gifts of new and powerful gods, and village life comes to turn on pleasing the gods in order to obtain more. The work of the community ceases as people wait on the beaches for more boats to arrive. Some of the more enthusiastic seekers of cargo may form a new priesthood and build wicker replicas of ships and airplanes to persuade the gods to return.

Many Westerners sense a similar loss of certainty. The advance of science, particularly evolutionary biology, has convinced intellectually honest believers that the first books of the Bible consist of an astute parable rather than an account of the origins of the world. Many of our religious institutions have been discredited, and others are slowly withering away. In such times, there is a great temptation to sit on the beach and wait for the great German theologian or the exotic swami to come across the water and sort things out for us. We are tempted to relieve anxieties by trying to relive the religious experiences of other places, other times, or other people. It is temptation to choke ourselves on esotericism, mimicry, or nostalgia. Instead, God wishes to visit us in our time and in our world, and he will restore us to his likeness within the context of our own lives.

(3) The Noonday Devil

In addition to clinging to what one possesses and grasping at what one does not yet possess, one may also despair of ever attaining them. Despair over attaining union with God can arise from two separate quarters. On one hand, we can see the divine likeness as something so different from ourselves that we lose hope of ever approaching it. On the other hand, it is possible to become jaded to the journey. That is to say, the practices associated with seeking the divine likeness become so routine that the joy and wonder drains out of the inward way.

Listlessness, depression, or a spiritual ennui appear in place of one's former enthusiasm, and one comes ever closer to abandoning the journey. The vice was so common in fourth century hermitages that the early Christian monks had a name for it: *accidie* (or *accidia*). In early monastic literature *accidie* is often depicted as a temptation of the early afternoon. By midday one's stamina wanes even though the evening's rest remains far away. One is vulnerable and easily discouraged. This, of course, is metaphor. While *accidie* may occur during the course of a single day, it may also visit us at any of those points on the inward journey at which we feel weary or especially tender. Yet even as *accidie* signals danger, it can also signal the advent of God's grace. Although it is almost a cliché to say that God never allows us to be tempted beyond our strength, it is nonetheless true. If we can welcome grace while tolerating *accidie*, the listlessness will eventually pass.

In its less virulent form *accidie* begins with nostalgia for what one has left behind. Moses' Israelites missed their onions and cucumbers. A cloistered nun might miss trips to the movies or the ball park. When I keep a vigil I miss sleeping. So the slippage begins. Nostalgia segues into regret, and regret metastasizes into despair. For example, I might be taken with a fit of nostalgia for my childhood days on the farm, regret that those days are over, and then make myself really miserable by telling myself that I will never see days like that again. Once one recognizes that nostalgia means slippage, this kind of *accidie* is easily remedied. The secret is to resist its beginnings. Rather than indulging in nostalgia, one simply continues with what one has been doing, and the temptation is eventually forgotten.

A second form of *accidie* is more dangerous. Paradoxically, as we draw closer to God we become increasingly aware of our own limitations and pettiness. We recognize that we have somehow gotten crosswise with God, and that we have lost the divine likeness. Simply put, we recognize that we are sinners and that the sin is repugnant. We become fed up with ourselves, and at this point one may attempt to eliminate the sin by eradicating the sinner. Now I am not talking about straightforward self-destructiveness here. This is a psychological problem and outside my bailiwick. Instead, I have in mind more subtle forms of self-abnegation which are not, at first sight, pathological.

A Sacrifice of Stolen Goods

Sometimes, the vice of self-abnegation masquerades as the virtue of selflessness. A friend of mine once decided to enter a Trappist monastery. Arriving at the abbey, he was overwhelmed by the beautiful architecture, the rolling farmlands, and the quiet. He saw monks rustling through the cloister in white robes, and he assumed that in such impressive company the best he could do would be to keep his mouth shut and to do what he was told. He stuck to this plan, and after a few months was deeply unhappy. He found that most of the time he was walking around in a vaguely angry mood. The reason, he discovered, was that he was forcing himself to be meek and docile at the expense of honesty and candor.

My friend is a bright fellow and does not suffer fools gladly. As long as I have known him he has demanded clarity and intellectual rigor from himself and from those around him. To his credit, he could never be satisfied with simple answers to complex questions. The monastic culture he found himself in did not look favorably on such a rigorously intellectual path toward God, and my friend tried to stifle his intellect in order to please his fellow monks.

For example, he tells me that a venerable and somewhat famous old monk once gave a talk which characterized a rather odd notion, astral projection, as dangerous. The reason, said the old monk, was because he had heard of a young man who had tried it with some success but who was unable to merge his soul back into his body and died. Now my friend was unwilling to swallow the idea that the young astral projectionist had performed the tantric equivalent of locking his keys inside his car. "I really wanted to ask him how it would be possible to confirm something like that," my friend later said. "After all, the only witness died during an alleged event which only he could confirm."

My friend became embittered because he kept trying to offer God and his monastic community what Saint Jerome used to call a sacrifice of stolen goods. God gave my friend a first rate mind, and by throttling it down my friend defeated the purpose of the gift. Because he was afraid to allow his intellect to flourish my friend became miserable, and his brother monks missed the opportunity to be challenged by it. The living God, who has a certain fondness for truth, was not well served. Instead, my friend continued to damp down his mind and blandly continence intellectual shabbiness. All the while he told himself that he was trying to learn humility and that the critical use of his mind was somehow self-serving. Unfortunately he had confused self-forgetful joy at being caught up in divine love, with self-abnegation, which is merely joyless resignation to the diminution of one's gifts. My friend got crosswise with God because he attempted to sacrifice the very thing God wanted him to nurture and use. He had to leave the monastery and enter graduate school before he felt genuinely at peace with himself.

Keeping One's Bearings

So much for the temptations of clinging to, grasping at, and rejecting God's gifts. In passive purgation God seeks to wean us away from these patterns of behavior so that we will be better able to glimpse him as he is. In the desert one's faith is reduced to its essentials, and because of this God's vital activity becomes more apparent. Yet just what transpires in the soul is not always clear to the individual. Consequently, it becomes important to seek sources of guidance and clarity. At least three sources of direction are available to those who find themselves on the purgative way. One may find one's direction in the desert by paying attention to the inner workings of the Holy Spirit, to one's own conscience, or one may be fortunate enough to find suitable mentors and companions.

When figuring out the state of one's soul, it is important to begin with one's own soul. God's grace visits each of us as we are in the present moment, and so the story of one's journey back to the divine likeness necessarily begins with this unique visitation. When a couple is in love, they will know more about their relationship than anyone else. Similarly, when someone begins to be caught up in divine love, the great authorities on that relationship will be God and that person. At the last supper Jesus assured his disciples that the divine presence would remain among them even when he was no longer physically present among them. "The Advocate, the Holy Spirit, whom the Father will send in my name, will teach you everything, and remind you of all that I have said to you" (John 14.26).

The gift of the Paraclete in one of the most remarkable of all the promises in sacred scripture. Through the Holy Spirit

God makes it possible for each of us to become one with him through love. This is no mere metaphor, but something quite real and quite palpable. By looking into the deeper parts of ourselves and by seeing love's work there, each of us may glimpse God's active, transformative presence. God already dwells within us, and by waking up to this reality we become one with him. Consequently, the chief way of finding a clear path through the desert is to follow the work of love within oneself. Whatever damps down this holy wonder is a cul-de-sac, and whatever fosters it points to our final destination. It is in this way that the Holy Spirit teaches everything.

Another desert guide is one's own conscience. "Conscience" is a much abused word. Since the early part of this century some have chosen to regard it as a sort of interior hall monitor busily jotting down and reporting violations of societal and religious taboos. Parents and Sunday school teachers abet this notion by convincing impressionable youngsters that conscience is "a little voice inside" which will keep them posted on what counts as a bad thing. Not surprisingly, by adolescence young people are more than ready to strip the bark off this officious little phoney. What has happened is that the moralists (as well as the teenage anti-moralists) tend to see action in accord with one's conscience as something which occurs at the periphery of one's personality. The little voice, or little enforcer, represents an external code of behavior which seems to have little to do with one's own inner life.

Fortunately, what often gets retailed as "conscience" has little to do with the real thing. Conscience is not something separate and alien to one's personality. Rather, the term "conscience" refers to the capacity for moral decisions of a healthy personality focused on a worthy goal. Action according to one's conscience consists in faithfulness to our most basic hopes and desires. It will entail a sincere love of God and neighbor, since it is through love that we find and are found by God. One may find one's bearings in the desert by asking oneself if the path ahead will realize one's hopes and enhance one's ability to love as God loves. If the path does not offer these possibilities, it is a dead end. On the other hand, if the path does offer one an opportunity to grow in faith, hope, and charity, it will certainly be worth exploring.

Often in the desert we are presented with more than one desirable path. In these instances, it is important to choose the path which fits most neatly with the trajectory of one's own life. In the eleventh century Saint Bernard of Clairvaux (1090–1153) went from village to village preaching about the heights of divine union which could be achieved in one of his order's monasteries. Women in these villages used to lock their husbands in the cellar to prevent them from hearing Bernard's sermons. In doing so, they did their husbands a great kindness. Rather than being tempted to run off to a monastery, their husbands would continue to have the opportunity to grow into the divine likeness in their homes and in their own villages. Rather than following a will-o'-the-wisp, they would live out the lives and commitments they had already made.

Community

If we are fortunate, we will find companions and mentors on the desert journey, and it is advisable to surround oneself with as many as possible. Such people will both support us when discouraged and keep us honest with ourselves.

Sometimes we may encounter people who are well along on the journey and teach us as much through their demeanor as by their words. These are forthrightly holy people who bring an atmosphere of joy and wonder to their surroundings. I suspect that the Zen poet Ryokan (1758–1831) was this sort of fellow. His poems are full of the kind joyful wonder that gives one permission to be oneself:

> A single path among ten thousand trees,
> A misty valley hidden among a thousand peaks.
> Not yet autumn but already leaves are falling;
> Not much rain but still the rocks grow dark.
> With my basket I hunt for mushrooms;
> With my bucket I draw pure spring water.
> Unless you got lost on purpose
> You would never get this far.[1]

It is best not to trouble such people with overly many questions about spirituality or about how to become one with God. They will not tell you any secrets because there are no secrets. Instead, observe how they live and how they see things, and be encouraged by their example. When my grandmother celebrated her ninety-fifth birthday, I asked her if she had any secrets for living to a ripe old age. "You just get here," she said. I asked her what I should be doing when I was ninety-five, and she replied, "Just what I'm doing, honey."

Sometimes, we may encounter learned or particularly clear-headed people. Although such people may not be so

---

1. Ryokan, *Dewdrops on a Lotus Leaf*, trans. John Stevens (Boston: Shambhala, 1993), 14.

far along on the path back to God as the forthrightly holy, they can offer us great insights into ourselves and into the nature of our journey. The learned can tell us about the adventures of other travelers and about what our destination might be like. The clear-headed can help us look at our lives dispassionately and help us sort out which of our desires come from God. I should add that clear-headed people are not always comfortable to be around. They insist on being honest with themselves, and they insist that those around them be equally truthful. They are masters at dispelling illusions and picking apart pretension. I have rarely felt comfortable when their talents have been directed at me, but I have never failed to benefit from them.

Finally, we may be fortunate enough to have good friends accompanying us on the way through the wilderness. When we are discouraged, they will assure us that we are indeed fighting the good fight, and good friends will take us to task if we are not. However, such friendships need not be based on across-the-board unanimity of opinion. In fact, a certain amount of disagreement tends to be both stimulating and a spur to honesty. For example, I have often gained much from conversations with Buddhist friends and from conversations with friends who have a more or a less rigorous approach to the Christian faith than my own. Similarly, a friend of mine likes to joke that the best marriages are those between spouses with incompatible vices.

Sheer Silence

As one advances along the purgative way prayer becomes a richer and more intimate experience and one's capacity to see the world as God sees it increases. Prior to embarking on the purgative way one's prayer involves many words and mental images, and often it has the character of communiques exchanged between sovereign states. For example, one may concentrate on transmitting a list of petitions to God and then sit back waiting to see whether the requests will be approved or denied. As one continues in the purgative way, however, one becomes increasingly aware of God's presence within oneself. One begins to seek out silence and solitude in order to be more attentive to this subtle presence, and one discovers that the divine presence is interwoven with one's own personality.

As our awareness of God's presence within us sharpens, our perspective on the world changes. Having tapped a source of joy and wonder within ourselves, the world around us now appears suffused with that same wonder. All is sustained by God's creative power, and now we sense ourselves connected to everything because of it. As we begin to sense the divine presence as it is woven into our own stream of consciousness, we begin to glimpse the world as God might see it and love it as he loves it. Eventually we discover that this union of God and our mental lives occurs through love and it is this same love which permeates all creation.

There is another Old Testament story about meeting God in the wilderness. In 1 Kings 19.1–18 we find the story of how Elijah escaped to the desert to avoid being liquidated by the political authorities and how he came to hear the voice of God. At first we see Elijah languishing on the periphery of the desert. He is worn out from his struggles with Israel's rulers, and waits for thirst or sword to put an end to the whole sorry business. Instead, the LORD sends an angel with food and water, and so strengthened Elijah walks deep into the desert to Mount Horeb, the place where, according to one tradition, God gave Moses the law. The LORD tells Elijah to be prepared for he will soon pass by that place. Elijah waits as winds, earthquakes, and fires—all traditional symbols of the divine presence—roll around on the mountain. But God is not present with any of these old messengers of his presence. Instead, the LORD appears within "the sound of sheer silence" and Elijah wraps his face in his cloak (1 Kings 19.12–13). Finally, in the new silence of the desert God is present.

Chapter 4

The Clear Light of God

*You never enjoy the world aright, till the Sea itself floweth
in your veins, till you are clothed with the heavens, and
crowned with the stars: and perceive yourself to be the
sole heir of the whole world, and more than so, because
men are in it who are every one sole heirs as well as
you. Till you can sing and rejoice and delight in God,
as misers do in gold, and Kings in scepters, you never enjoy the
world.*
—Thomas Traherne, *Centuries,* I.29

The Illuminative Way

Once we owned a cat named Nora who seemed to have
set up shop at a middling level on the ascent to God. Placid
and fat, Nora spent her mornings lying in a pool of sunlight
near the back door, and sometimes she gazed into the distance as if she were seeing something of great importance
hidden from the rest of us. Then she would pad away from
the door to dip water from the toilet or present us with a hair
ball. For these reasons I decided that Nora had arrived at the
feline equivalent of the illuminative way. Among humans,
illumination marks that phase on the journey back to the

divine likeness at which active and passive purgation begin to bear fruit. At the onset of illumination one enjoys a more vivid sense of God's presence and, for a while, savors some of the results of the desert journey. However, the ultimate embrace of God is still to come.

As we have seen, the purgative way is a kind of exercise program for the soul, and the desert, be it an actual wilderness or its functional equivalent, is the gymnasium in which the training takes place. As the soul's training continues, one becomes more oneself and thereby better able to discern and approach the divine presence. The chief characteristic of the illuminative way is a heightened awareness of God's presence which comes about as the capacities of one's personality come habitually to be directed toward what is most real and genuinely human.

To use another metaphor, illumination corresponds to the moment at which runners find their stride. The healthy exercise continues, but now a rhythm is established through which one is caught up in the toil itself. The journey through the wilderness continues but now stands revealed as, essentially, a journey to where God dwells in the most central parts of oneself. As God's grace percolates through one's personality, it becomes possible both to glimpse more of the divine nature and to participate in it.

Characteristics of the Illuminative Way

As illumination progresses, one gains a fresh and vivid sense of being grasped by God, and now all things seem transfused with his presence. Ordinary things now hum with a half-hidden divinity, and one senses oneself expanding in response to this newfound beauty. Gerard Manley Hopkins's sonnet *God's Grandeur* expresses something of this new-found consciousness:

> The world is charged with the grandeur of God.
> It will flame out, like shining from shook foil;
> It gathers to a greatness, like the ooze of oil
> Crushed. Why do men then now not reck his rod?
>
> Generations have trod, have trod, have trod;
> And all is seared with trade; bleared, smeared with toil;
> And wears man's smudge and shares man's smell: the soil
> Is bare now, nor can foot feel, being shod.
>
> And for all this, nature is never spent;
> There lives the dearest freshness deep down in things;
> And though the last lights off the black West went
> Oh, morning, at the brown brink eastward springs—
> Because the Holy Ghost over the bent
> World broods with warm breast and with ah! bright wings.

Another lovely metaphor for God's creative and sustaining activity is the vision of the sixth century monastic reformer Benedict of Nursia (480–547). Legend tells us that once while keeping a vigil Saint Benedict saw a ray of light shining from the hand of God. Suspended within the one ray Benedict saw all creation whirling in the golden light like flecks of dust.

More than merely sensing that all creation is sustained by God's ongoing creative activity, those entering upon the illuminative way find themselves caught up in the whirling dance in the golden light. Now the great secret is revealed: the same power which sustains the created order is also at work within oneself insofar as one is part of that order. As the first book of the Bible says, "God saw everything that he had made, and indeed, it was very good" (Genesis 1.31). Now for the first time the Christian mystic takes to heart the meaning of these words. Because of this, preeminent experience on the illuminative way is wonder. One marvels at one's surroundings, and one marvels at what lies within. From wonder comes love and, through love, oneness with God.

The Relatively Unimportant Matter of Mystical Phenomena

The early phases of illumination are sometimes accompanied by certain sensory phenomena, and I suspect that this is more common than is generally recognized. Nevertheless, such experiences are no more evidence of especial holiness than they are of mental instability. Rather, the sensory phenomena encountered from time to time on the illuminative way are simply what one might expect given that God actively seeks each of us and meets us in the ways in which we are best able to receive him. Should someone have such an experience, the important thing is not the perceptual content itself but, instead, the presence of God which underwrites that experience.

Let me give just one example of such a sensory experience and make a few observations about it before getting on with the real business of this chapter. During his senior year of college at a large midwestern university a friend of mine had a rather engaging experience of the presence of God. While on a Holy Week retreat my friend found himself sitting alone in a small chapel. He sensed a deep stillness both in himself and in his surroundings, and he sat with his eyes closed enjoying it. After a while, he was no longer conscious of the passage of time but only of the stillness. Then it seemed as though someone had slipped into the chapel and had begun burning a subtle and beautiful-smelling incense. When he opened his eyes, the chapel was empty, but it seemed bathed in a clear golden light which made everything around him appear distinct and richly colored.

While such an experience has a certain charm to it, it is even better simply to experience being loved and sustained by God. Such simple awareness is more direct. Suppose that a friend and I decided to wash some very dirty windows, and that we decided that he would work on the outside and I on the inside. Initially, I would perceive him only as a vague blur through the dusty, fly-spotted glass. However, as we scrubbed our respective sides of the window it would become easier to see one another, and if we did our jobs right the glass would become virtually invisible.

The purgative way is something like washing windows. One works with God to cultivate and mature the senses, the emotions, and the intellect in order to make them fit instruments for divine love. Initially, the clear light of God's presence may light up our faculties in various interesting and beautiful ways, and so beginners might find themselves enjoying, for example, unfamiliar sensory experiences. However, such experiences usually indicate that God's presence is still being blocked or refracted at the more superficial levels of one's personality. The senses, emotions, and intellect are not yet translucent, and so the sensory phenomena of the illuminative way mark of God's presence in the soul even as they occlude it. As someone progresses along the purgative way awareness of God's presence becomes more immediate because it is no longer refracted at the surface levels of consciousness.

Those who experience some sort of sensory phenomena should by all means enjoy them. But remember: they are less important than they seem. As God's light shines into the soul, it may light up the senses insofar as perception is one of many capacities of the soul. However, God wants to get at and live in the innermost portions of our personalities, deeper even than those parts of us which traffic in words, images, pleasures, or pains. God is a courteous visitor and will be pleased to be invited even onto the front porch of the soul, but it is best to welcome him as deeply into ourselves as possible. Once God has become at home in the deeper parts of our personalities, ordinary life itself will seem infused with wonders, and unusual sensory experiences will be superfluous and may even seem a bit overdone.

Sensory and seemingly miraculous experiences are neither as deep nor as significant as they appear, and it is not productive to go out of one's way seeking them. If such experiences happen to occur, all well and good, but if we become obsessed with seeking or causing them, then we are no longer seeking God with undivided minds. A Zen master named Ikkyu (1394–1481) once met a magician who chided him for being unable to produce miracles. "On the contrary," Ikkyu responded, "in Zen everyday acts are miracles." Unimpressed, the magician performed an elaborate ritual and summoned up a fiery image of a fierce divinity. Then he challenged Ikkyu to perform an even mightier work. Ikkyu replied, "Here's a miracle issuing from my own body," and promptly relieved himself on the apparition reducing it to a pile of soggy ashes.[1]

---

1. See John Stevens, *Three Zen Masters* (Tokyo: Kodansha International, 1993), 32–33.

Does Simple Awareness of God's Presence Prove Anything?

On more than one occasion, I have had a distinct sense of being loved or sustained by God. However, at these times I have also wondered whether or not the experience was genuine. After all, my imagination is more than capable of convincing me that I am absolutely safe, that my small life in this little town fits into a larger plan, or of many other things that I would dearly love to be true. Moreover, my belief that I am being sustained by God does not seem to have the same obvious and tangible justification as, say, my belief that the cabbages in my garden are infested with slugs. I can easily confirm my beliefs about my cabbages by going out to the garden and looking at them. My experience of God's presence, however, seems not to be susceptible to the same sort of direct confirmation. Thus, at first sight, my beliefs about my cabbages seem more certain than my beliefs about my relationship with God.

It took me a long time to realize that I was not thinking clearly either about my experiences of God's presence or my perceptual experiences. Let's start with the cabbages and slugs. If I see slimy brown insects oozing across the beautiful blue-green leaves, then I take it that my fears for my cabbages have come true. This belief is founded upon assumptions I have about how the world hangs together. For example, though I am never surprised to find slugs clinging to my cabbages, I would be astounded to find chocolate eclairs. The reason is that I have plenty of reasonable expectations about how the physical world will present itself to me, and it regularly lives up to them. I expect to find bugs in my garden, not French pastries. There is, of course, nothing about holding such expectations that impedes hard-headed, rational thought. In fact, one implicit, rational expectation is that my sense-experiences will be comprehensible and similar to previous experiences.

As someone trying to live as a Christian, I have made even more assumptions about the nature of reality. To begin with, I assume that there is more to creation than can be encountered in three dimensions by the five senses. Further, I assume that God is always at work seeking each of us. After all, every Sunday I stand up with my cohorts in Episcopalianism and recite the Nicene Creed. The Creed states that God created both visible and invisible things and that Christ became incarnate for our salvation. Since I publicly claim to have these expectations, I really shouldn't be surprised when I have experiences conforming to them. For example, if I already believe that prayer is possible, I shouldn't be shocked when I see it working. Moreover, if I believe that God transcends the human mind and is something other than a physical object, it should come as no surprise that I feel his presence in a different way than I sense the presence of slugs among my cabbages.

My point is that a rough-and-ready empiricism is unsatisfactory for evaluating experiences of God's presence. Although it is quite easy to confirm my beliefs about my cabbage patch by looking at it, a fleeting awareness of God's presence will probably not register on my sense organs at all. If I were to take sensation as the standard for all genuine experiences, then I would have to conclude that many of my experiences of God were unreliable or illusory. However, as a believer I have expectations which draw me beyond the limits of merely physical perception. Insofar as I hold these expectations consistently, there will be nothing irrational in my claim that I have perceived God's presence.

This is not to say that one's experience of God's presence will be sufficient to convince a non-believer of the truth of the Gospel. Converting a non-believer is a different sort of project than encouraging a believer to be consistent in his or her beliefs. It is, after all, only through one's status as a believer that an intimation of God's presence makes sense at all. For a religious experience to be more than just a curiosity, it must be seen from the inside, from the believer's point of view. This is why it is not fitting for me as a believer to judge an experience of God's presence by the same set of expectations by which I would judge my beliefs about physical phenomena. I have already committed myself to an additional set of standards, and it would be inconsistent on my part suddenly to abandon them.

Discursive and Contemplative Prayer

Having come to see with the eyes of faith, it makes perfect sense to say that prayer is both possible and efficacious. Moreover, if prayer is possible and efficacious, it might be a very good idea to do it often. The remainder of this chapter will be about what has traditionally been called discursive prayer, that is, prayer which traffics in either interior or public words and images. The next chapter will deal with contemplative prayer, that is, prayer which does not rely on words or images but rather consists in inner stillness and the quiet enjoyment of the divine presence. In both this chapter and the next I hope to provide a few practical suggestions about how to pray. However, the reader should be aware that the real teacher of prayer is the Holy Spirit. At best, I can only make a few suggestions about how to become aware of the inner work of the Spirit. Prayer itself is something better done than described.

The Lord's Prayer

When Jesus's disciples asked him how to pray, he taught them the Lord's Prayer (Luke 11.1–4; Matthew 6.9–13). Let us get this much straight right from the beginning: the Lord's Prayer does not consist of a set of words that God wants to hear repeated at regular intervals, and it is not a set of protocols for establishing or conducting relations with the divinity. Instead, the Lord's Prayer sets out a number of attitudes without which a loving relationship with God cannot flourish. The Lord's Prayer shows us how to enter into the divine presence, but it isn't intended to be used as a script once we get there.

First, the Lord's Prayer reminds us that God created us, that God takes an intense interest in each of us, and that it is possible to approach God with the same familiarity with which children approach their parents. Then the prayer reminds us that our origins and purpose extend beyond the limits imposed by space and time. Next, it asks that God's presence may be manifest in creation, that all people will find that presence accessible, and that the earth will become like heaven.

Only after seeking God's blessing for the whole of creation does the focus of the Lord's Prayer shift to individual needs. Having identified oneself with the expansiveness of God's grace, one now asks for God's sustenance for the coming day. Notice that the petition is not that one be sustained for a year or a month but for the coming day only. Although God's grace will always sustain us it nonetheless is important to ask regularly so as not to take it lightly.

Then one asks to be forgiven according to the standard by which one forgives. In Greek, the word used is *aphiemi*, and a more literal translation would be "toss aside." If we are locked into a self-stoking cycle of hurting and getting hurt, it will be difficult, if not impossible, to get on with the real business of life, that is, getting caught up in the love of God which percolates through the whole created order. Resentment, cruelty, and recrimination are not germane to a life lived honestly, fully, and joyously. If we find ourselves caught-up in a cycle of hurting and getting hurt, the only way out is to toss the pain and the desire to cause pain aside and begin again to be caught up in God's love.

The Lord's Prayer concludes with petitions that one be drawn toward God and away from temptation and the power of evil. That it is desirable to be delivered from evil is self-evident. However, it is less clear why one would not want to be tested. In fact, some people often claim that untested virtue is nonexistent. Yet as we stand before God in prayer, the point is not to revel in our virtue but to welcome the advent of grace. Next to God's goodness, all our well-tried virtues would seem as thin as the gold plate on a Las Vegas wedding ring. The only respectable stance one can take before God is that of plain honesty and openness. This is true humility.

The Lord's Prayer shows that a substantial relationship with God is marked by confidence, expansiveness, humility, and a desire to see grace manifest in all creation. But just how does one begin, and how does one progress? In the first place, if one desires to pray, then the conversation has already begun—and it was God who initiated it. The desire for God is, in fact, a response to the Holy Spirit who is already at work within us. The first move on one's own part, whatever move that might be, will be a response in a conversation already begun by the inner prompting of the Holy Spirit. There is no reason to worry about how to begin praying; a desire for God's presence shows that prayer has already begun.

Common Prayer

One makes progress in prayer by becoming better able to respond to God's presence. There are several ways of becoming attentive to the divine presence, but perhaps the surest is to surround oneself with people who share a similar purpose. It is important not to underestimate Christ's promise that "where two or three are gathered in my name, I am there among them" (Matthew 18.20). For what it is worth, the true presence of Christ among assembled believers is one of the few doctrines which has never been widely disputed during the long and contentious history of debate about the content of the Christian faith.

Many of my friends who are not regular church goers point out that God is everywhere insofar as his creative activity sustains and permeates the whole world. They seek God in forests and on mountain trails up above timberline and argue that the creator is most easily glimpsed in what is best and most noble in his creation. I cannot argue with success; God's presence is evident in places of great natural beauty and only the most jaded could miss it. There is a wonderful sort of chamber music among a few friends enjoying the outdoors together, and even someone hiking alone in the forest is like a single instrument playing a simple melody. I have no doubt that God's presence sounds in experiences of this type, for I have heard it myself.

Yet I am also fond of going to the symphony. In fact, I would almost pay the whole price of a ticket to hear the orchestra tune. First, the oboe plays a single A. The first violin picks it up, and soon the whole orchestra is humming with the note. Then there is silence as the conductor steps to the podium and raps it a couple times with his baton. Now the music begins, and the hall fills with the score's ordered fluidity. Each instrument contributes its part to the score as its sound is gathered up into a single greater sound first heard only in the composer's mind.

A healthy worshiping community is something like a symphony orchestra in that it should allow us both to express the unique aspects of our lives and to be caught up in something greater than ourselves. A very ancient Christian document called the *Didache* expresses a similar understanding of common prayer. For the anonymous second century writer, the gathered community became something more than the sum of its parts in the same way that gathered grain transcends its parts when it is baked into a loaf of bread. For the anonymous writer, such was the great secret and deeper significance of the Lord's Supper.

> As to the Eucharist, give thanks in this way: First, over the cup say, 'Our Father, we give you thanks for the holy vine of David your child which you made known to us through Jesus your child. To you be glory through all ages.' Over the broken bread say 'Our Father, we give you thanks for the life and knowledge which you have made known to us through Jesus your child. To you be glory through all the ages. Just as this broken bread was scattered upon the mountains and was brought together to become one, so may your church be brought together from the ends of the earth into your kingdom. For glory and power is yours through all the ages.'[2]

---

2. *Didache* 9.1–4 (my translation).

According to the author of the *Didache*, those engaged in common prayer are, through Christ, gathered up into God's kingdom.

Common prayer is both a group project and a very personal experience. When I make my yearly retreat at the monastery, I particularly enjoy listening to the monks sing the psalms. All the monks wear white robes, and at a distance they look much the same. Once they begin singing, however, their uniqueness becomes apparent. The novices look rapt and attentive. A brother who has been in the monastery for many years grins and sways to the ancient melody while younger monks discreetly roll their eyes at his behavior. The abbot and prior affect the deadpan expressions expected of those in authority. Yet all, to the extent that they are willing, seem caught up in the common project of standing before God as one.

Similarly, if one has lived in a small town parish for a number of years, one can see the liturgy settling down into people's lives. Ragged copies of the *Book of Common Prayer* or the threadbare velvet of an elderly warden's doctoral hood give quiet testimony to years of liturgical perseverance. One may observe an acquaintance's lips pressed tightly together during the Creed as she struggles with her faith and then, a couple years later, see her speaking the words and recognize that a crisis has been weathered honestly. A married couple clasp hands during the Lord's Prayer and smile at forgiveness freely given and freely accepted. Common prayer lends an order and structure to one's life as a member of a community. It marks births, marriages, and deaths. Sometimes the Sunday liturgy sets the tone for the rest of the week, and some Christian traditions use liturgical prayer to order the hours of every day.

We live in a cynical age, but I suspect that God is encountered more often at regular Sunday services than many realize. In a good worshiping community one will likely find companions on the journey toward God and traditions and practices proven to make the journey easier. After a while, one also discovers that one no longer belongs just to one's own era. As Christians we believe in the communion of saints. That is, we believe that the human family is making a common pilgrimage toward God and that this journey has now been going on for several millennia. Many Christians believe that the dead are with God and even now are enjoying his presence. It is, at least, plausible that such souls continue to have a concern for those of us who have not yet found our way so entirely into God's presence.

Scriptural Prayer

Another good place to seek depth at prayer is in scripture. When we pick up the Bible to pray, some things will no longer be relevant. In the first place, opening the Bible to pray means seeking God's presence in its pages. The emphasis will be on having an experience of God, not on checking facts or assembling proof texts for pet theories. There is, of course, a time and place for such things, but it is not here and not now. Instead, the point is to read oneself into scripture, to assimilate the Bible's stories and ideas into one's own personality and way of life.

For example, suppose someone praying the book of the prophet Amos arrived at 8.4–7 and the words:

Hear this, you who trample on the needy,
  and bring ruin to the poor of the land,

saying, 'When will the new moon be over and the Sabbath,
     so that we may offer wheat for sale?
We will make the ephah small and the shekel great,
     and practice deceit with false balances,
buying the poor for silver and the needy for a pair of
sandals,
     and selling the sweepings of the wheat.'
The LORD has sworn by the pride of Jacob:
     'Surely I will never forget any of their deeds.'

Remember, our friend is trying to have a direct experience of God through the sacred text. Unless our friend is a rather unique character, it will not be pertinent to her prayer either to ponder eighth-century Israelite economic arrangements or even to become exercised on behalf of the eighth-century Israelite poor. The former is errant speculation and the latter antiquarian sentimentality.

On the other hand, suppose she asked herself, "Does this kind of exploitation go on around here, and am I in collusion with it?" Now our friend finds God addressing her directly, and she may well find herself pushed toward specific kinds of action. She might find herself called to research which companies have exploitative business practices and to cease investing in these firms. She might find herself called to allow her employees to make a living rather than just the minimum wage, or she might feel called to become a hard-boiled union organizer. She might even find herself called to spend less time making money and more time appreciating the life she already has. In any case, we will see her drawing closer to the divine likeness as her life and the world of scripture merge.

This Is Canaan

One of my favorite scenes of people praying with scripture occurred about four blocks from our home about a hundred and thirty years ago. On an autumn afternoon in 1867, a crowd assembled to lay the cornerstone of Calvary Episcopal Church. Inside the cornerstone they placed a handful of coins, some tracts on the evils of drink, and a copy of the *Book of Common Prayer*. Then the Right Reverend George Randall, first Episcopal bishop of the Colorado Territory, preached a sermon on Genesis 28.17: "How dreadful is this place! This is none other than the house of God, and this is the gate of heaven" (KJV). I have never been able to uncover the manuscript, but it must have been quite a sermon.

In 1867, Golden was a barren, isolated boom town. Teamster wagons trucked supplies in from St. Joseph, Missouri, four weeks and seven hundred miles away. Our town lay in a valley so dry and treeless that those who planted trees got their names printed in the newspaper. Yet if the distances and arid climate were unnerving to newcomers from back east, there was also great natural beauty and the hope of making a decent living farming, selling dry goods, or working in the mines. As the Civil War ended veterans of the Union Army found their way out here and began to build a city. A municipal bridge replaced the privately-owned old toll bridge over Clear Creek, farmers dug irrigation ditches, and in October the Episcopalians set to work on their red brick Gothic chapel. Bishop Randall must have sensed the interwoven hope and unease of his congregation. Perhaps felt it himself.

When the Episcopalians laid their corner stone Bishop Randall chose to preach on a lesson from the cycle of stories about the ancient patriarch Jacob. After prevailing in a

quarrel with his brother, Jacob journeyed into a new country and camped for the night. During the night he dreamed
of a ladder extending from earth to heaven and of angels
going up and down it. He dreamed that God would be with
him and give a new territory to him and to his decedents.
When he awoke, Jacob exclaimed that he had found himself
in an awesome place and proceeded to build a shrine (see
Genesis 28.10–18). Clearly, Bishop Randall meant for his
flock to view themselves as latter day Jacobs and Rachels.
Like ancient Bethel, nineteenth century Golden was a fearsome and wonderful place, and those who came here
invoked the God of the patriarchs.

A Method for Private Scriptural Prayer

Since the Middle Ages those interested in praying the
Bible have been advised, as the *Book of Common Prayer* says,
to begin by reading, marking, and inwardly digesting the
sacred text. The first step is entirely commonsensical. If one
wants to pray with a scriptural story, it makes good sense to
find out what that story really says, and the best way to do
that is to read it for oneself. Find a quiet, private spot and
slowly read through a bit of the Bible. The focus is not on
completing a set amount of reading or furthering one's edu-
cation but, rather, to meander through the text in God's
presence. It is a time for leisurely enjoying the Bible's words
and images as they unfold in the mind.

Next, one allows one's mind to light on a particular idea,
phrase, or image. As the ancient Christians would have said,
having broken the bread of scripture, it is now time to chew
and swallow it. For example, suppose someone were reading
Matthew 13.45:

Again, the kingdom of heaven is like a merchant in search of fine pearls; on finding one pearl of great value, he went and sold all that he had and bought it.

She might begin by asking herself what her own pearl of great value might be and if she is sure enough of her judgment or brave enough to sacrifice everything in order to obtain it. She might imagine herself as the merchant holding the cool, lucid pearl in the palm of her hand wondering what to do next. The point is to explore the ideas, metaphors, and emotions of the story and to incorporate them into one's own inner life in whatever ways one finds comfortable and effective.

Sometimes it helps to use one's imagination when marking and inwardly digesting the sacred text. For instance, someone reading a miracle story might imagine its setting, populate it with a cast of characters, set the whole thing in motion, and watch it like mental television. But there is no reason to stop there. One might imagine oneself as one or another of the characters, imagine interviewing one or another of the characters, or even having a conversation with Christ himself. Here, however, I am reporting other people's experiences. While other people seem to have no trouble imagining palm trees, dromedaries, and a cast of thousands, I tend to give up after a quarter of an hour having managed to summon up only a single palm tree. Nonetheless, I wish you, dear reader, the best of luck.

Having meandered through the text and pondered its words and images, one now turns toward God. Our friend praying about the pearl of great price might say, "The people who love me are all pearls of great value. Lord, please help me treasure them and help them to flourish." On the other hand, she might not address any words to God but simply acknowledge the divine presence and continue thinking of specific ways of helping her loved ones flourish. In any case, the important thing is to use mental words and images, specifically those of scripture, in drawing close to God. Explicitly or implicitly, one engages in a dialogue with God thanking him for what has been received, asking for what is needed by oneself or others, seeking his will in a particular situation, or offering oneself to his service.

Finally, the prayer will become simple. At first, someone praying with scripture might sense God's presence, address words to that presence, and assign words to the sensed reply. But eventually the words become heavy, blunt instruments which cannot dig down to the roots of the experience. One's standard range of emotions and bodily sensations seem too coarse to get to the heart of things. Instead, one feels caught up in God and perceives that God is getting at features of one's personality deeper than words, images, emotions, of bodily sensations. Prayer with words and images segues into contemplative prayer, that is, simple attentiveness to the divine presence.

I will discuss contemplative prayer in detail in the next chapter. For the moment, it will be sufficient to make a few remarks about why an inability to use words or images during prayer does not count as a failure at prayer. In the past, particularly among Protestant congregations, people had the idea that prayer should be a quantifiable activity. Petitions had to be delivered, thanksgivings made, apologies said, and offerings of oneself to God's service tendered. Quite often, such prayer took the form of long strings of mental words broadcast to a distant divinity. If producing such a broadcast turned tedious, then one simply exercised a little self-discipline and did it some more. Yet prayer is part of one's relationship with God, and loving relationships rarely have meters strapped to them. Just as it is absurd to take the minutes at a birthday party, it makes no sense to be standoffish and formal when God has other things in mind.

One of the great scandals in the history of humanity's dealings with God was the loss of the divine name. The third chapter of Exodus tells of the LORD sending Moses back into Egypt to lead the children of Israel to freedom. When Moses asks who he should say sent him, God tells Moses his name, a word derived from the Hebrew verb meaning "to be" (Exodus 3.13–15). The ancient Hebrews rarely used God's name because they believed that knowing someone's name gave one power over that person, and they did not want to be uppity with God. Unfortunately, they were so meek that over the centuries the correct pronunciation and spelling of God's name were forgotten. Although God had freely given Moses his name, excessive reverence allowed it to be forgotten. For us, the moral of this sad story is that if we feel drawn to contemplative prayer, the most likely explanation is that God desires that we pray in this way, and actually doing so will be the most fittingly reverent response.

Some Other Ways of Praying

Scripture need not be the exclusive starting point for Christian prayer. Just as God's concern for humanity may be discerned in the books of the Old and New Testaments, God's continuing sustenance of all that is stands revealed in the book of nature. I remember a morning in late June when

I stood in my garden smelling the damp earth and watching the sun crest above the cliffs of Table Mesa. The corn and beans had reached that stage at which they are no longer tender but not yet fruitful, and raindrops still clung to their leaves. The pea vines draped themselves heavily over their sticks and held up a profusion of pods and white blooms. I bent to pull a few weeds, and when I came to the raspberries I found a single red fruit clinging to one of the canes. It was the first of the season, and its smell and taste were just right. For a moment, perhaps, I glimpsed the world as God desires it to be, a place both fresh and full of promise.

Similarly, art or music can draw us closer to God. An icon shimmering behind its lamp draws not only the senses but the whole mind into that which it represents. For a moment, it might seem that one is gazing not into painted eyes but into the eyes of the Savior, the Virgin, or the Baptizer. A penitente crucifix in a small adobe chapel might draw the mind from that representation of a particular moment of suffering toward an appreciation of the scope of the world's pain and of God's desire that it be redeemed. A choir singing Monteverdi's Vespers might put one in mind of the richness of creation and of God's desire that all things flourish, or an orchestra playing one of Shostakovich's symphonies might encourage someone to endure inner chaos and to continue seeking God even though he seems absent.

As one progresses along the illuminative way, prayer and the activities of day-to-day life begin to fuse. An awareness of God's presence begins to follow one from the place one happened to be praying to the kitchen, the bus, or the computer keyboard. Thus begins what has been traditionally called the practice of the presence of God. Once one begins to experience the fact that the whole world is God's, it becomes impossible to confine one's relationship with God to just one compartment of one's life. Arbitrary distinctions between the sacred and profane melt away, and one comes to turn toward God habitually. One prays not only at the times set for prayer but in the intervening moments as well. Living becomes praying, and everything encountered through the senses gets taken up in that prayer. Now one moves through the world with an abiding awareness of God's presence, an awareness by which one may be caught up in God both on Sunday morning at church and on Monday evening preparing supper.

Chapter 5

Contemplation

Senses cannot resemble that which they cannot apprehend; nor express that which they cannot resemble, but in a shady manner. But man is made in the Image of God, and is therefore a mirror and representative of Him. And therefore in himself he may see God, which is his glory and felicity. His love can extend to all objects . . . contemplate the beauty, enjoy the benefit, and reign over all it sees and enjoys like the Eternal Godhead.
—Thomas Traherne, *Centuries*, I.23

Attentive Stillness

Once the warm nights of May arrive, Barbara and I go to a dilapidated amusement park on the shores of a small lake. We walk out on a pier to toss popcorn to chubby carp and dodge the North Denver kids who dash from ride to ride. At dusk the management switches on the lights, and the park hums and whirls with thousands of colored bulbs. But few things are more delicious than the summer's first roller coaster ride. We pile into the cars and coast through a broad tunnel smelling of creosote. When we emerge, a big chain's teeth grab the bottoms of the cars and begin dragging us up the first hill. Pasted to the back of the seat, I listen to the chain's metallic clicks and smell the night air. Then comes *the moment.* No longer gripped by the metal teeth, the cars pause for half a heartbeat at the top of the hill and then again begin to move.

Eventually prayer leads to similar crucial moments. Those seeking God often happen onto a silent, still anticipation in which they glimpse God not through their senses, emotions, or intellect but in spite of them. This is something more to be experienced than written or read about. It is a real, palpable experience, but words cannot describe it any more than they can get to the heart of what it is to smell an antique rose or taste a wild strawberry. At best, the words point us in the direction of the prayer of quiet or circumscribe its boundaries. Words and images can tell us that God is most decisively met with in the silence of the soul, that wonder and abiding joy await us there, or that having had such an experience one will want to repeat it. Beyond this, I can only encourage readers to seek the experience and suggest that it will be much as they suspected it might be.

The Mystical Mountain

Four hundred years ago, a Spanish mystic drew a picture of a mountain to represent the soul's ascent to God through prayer. At the summit he placed simple stillness in the divine presence, and around it he wrote: "Nothing, nothing, nothing, nothing, nothing, nothing, and even on the Mount nothing."[1] It was not the nothing of non-existence the mystic had in mind but the nothing of ineffabil-

---

1. John of the Cross, *The Ascent of Mount Carmel* in *The Collected Works of St. John of the Cross*, ed. Kieran Kavanaugh and Otilio Rodriguez (Washington D.C.: ICS Publications, 1979): 66–67.

ity, that is, the paralysis of the human intellect when confronted with God's grandeur. Here is an illustration. If in deepest January someone asked me what I had just planted in my garden, I would reply, "nothing." In this case, I would mean only that I had not scratched any seeds into the barren ground. But suppose somebody asked me what I knew about how chemists make the artificial banana flavor in salt water taffy, and I replied, "nothing." In this instance, I would not mean that such knowledge did not exist but only that I did not possess it. I would have meant that there were limits to my knowledge of the subject, not limits to subject itself.

Similarly, when one reaches the top of the Spanish mystic's mountain and finds "nothing," it is not God's absence that is experienced but, rather, his majesty. We may assume that we have discovered the limits of that part of ourselves that traffics in words and images, and that now is being drawn beyond them. In what is often called contemplation, God draws us beyond the bounds of the usual modes of thought and perception, and so it should come as no surprise that the experience cannot be described in these terms. When God begins to draw us into intimate communion with himself, our natural powers of perception and thought are not fit to encompass or grasp him. Instead, in half a heartbeat God grasps us at the center of our personalities and begins drawing us inward and into himself. Such is the prayer of quiet.

Loving with Heart, Soul, and Mind

Before we go further, I need to make a handful of persnickety but vital clarifications. Prayer consists in responding to God's grace and in coming to know him more intimately. As such, it fulfills the first part of Christ's command to love God with all one's heart, soul, and mind (see Matthew 22.36–38). Unfortunately, the terms "love," "heart," "soul," and "mind" have become such blunt tools that I can say little of substance until I have sharpened them and attempted to restore some of their original power. When the words mean something again, then I can gesture toward what is more important: that moment in prayer at which words give way to a purer and more intimate awareness of God.

Let us begin with how the words "heart" and "mind" are used in plain English. The heart is an organ in the center of the chest which pumps oxygen-carrying blood to all the other parts of the living body. Without oxygenated blood, we die. So in a very literal sense, the heart is the central and most crucial feature of one's physical being. Now let us look at how the word "mind" is commonly used. Sometimes on a crowded bus or in a busy cafeteria, someone will say, "Do you mind if I sit here?" Occasionally young clerks are left to "mind the shop," and, of course, we are all familiar with the shepherds who were minding their flocks by night. In these cases, "minding" is much more than the detached clicking of mental machinery. Instead, the word points to an engaged attentiveness which precedes activity. Clerks mind the shop to ring up customers. Shepherds mind their flocks to protect them from coyotes, and if someone does mind my sitting next to him on the bus, I stay clear of him.

The same rules are at work in New Testament Greek. "Heart" (*kardia*) denotes the central aspect of physical life, and "mind" (*dianoia*) denotes the capacity for taking interest in and paying attention to one's surroundings. Notice that neither in English nor in Greek are "heart" and "mind" synonyms for "emotions" and "intellect." While it may be the case that our hearts flutter when we are startled or pound when we are angry, this is obviously not the same thing as experiencing the emotions. After all, one's heart may also pound after riding a bicycle to the top of a hill or flutter when one catches sight of a sweetheart. Instead, the word "heart" has more to do with the central features of our physiology than it does with emotions which may, or may not, leave traces there. "*Kardia*" means "heart," and designates, first of all, the central organ of the living body. Similarly, both "*dianoia*" and "mind" have more to do with taking interest in things than with detached pondering. Taken literally, the word "*dianoia*" means "awareness of what surrounds one." So here's the payoff: heart and mind are not mutually hostile bits of the personality but complementary and crucial components of a whole, embodied person.

Another much-abused word is "soul." Most of us are used to seeing the word "soul" contrasted with the word "body" and to hearing talk about how and why the soul is something separate from the body. Such dichotomy mongering often leads to the idea that the soul is to the body as a bus driver is to a bus. Just as a driver climbs into a bus in the morning and steers it along its route, it is sometimes alleged that souls hop into bodies and steer them around for seventy or eighty years. Yet if this were the case, there would be no point to Christ's resurrection. It would have been sufficient for Jesus to have imparted his teaching to the apostles and to have returned to a disembodied state having made a point or two about self-control and mastery of the flesh. Instead, Christ's incarnation tells us that our own bodies are holy and noble, and his resurrection shows that we will enter eternity in the flesh (see Job 19.26; 1 Corinthians 15.35–55).

The Greek word for "soul" is "*psyche*." Literally translated, it means "breath." In Latin, the corresponding word is "*spiritus*" from which we get the English words "spirit" and "respiration." There is a similar word in Hebrew, "*nefesh*," which may be translated as "breath," "life," "soul," or even as "person." This is the word, for example, used in Exodus 12.37 to refer to the six hundred thousand Moses led up out of the land of Egypt.

Breathing fascinated the ancients because it seemed to be something belonging both to the physical and spiritual orders. On one hand, breath is usually invisible and is, to a certain extent, under one's conscious control. In this sense, breath seemed not to be subject to the necessities of material creation. On the other hand, breathing is something that living bodies perform with the aid of their physical equipment. In this sense, it seemed to belong to the material order. Thus, the Greek word for "soul" denotes something poised between two worlds, something that accounts for the difference between a living body and a corpse. The point of all this is that the English word "soul" properly refers to the first principle of physical existence. The soul is not a wan ghost pulling the body's strings. Rather, the soul is that mysterious force within us which is responsible for our being alive at all.

Similarly, my own experience indicates that soul and body are more intimately entwined than is generally acknowledged. For instance, before I began writing this morning I had two stiff cups of coffee, and even now, several hours later, I am still noticing their effect. Last night Barbara and I had a late dinner on the patio. A glass of red wine, the splashing of water in the creek, the warm brick on my bare feet, vegetables from our garden, and a certain sparkle in Barbara's hazel eyes all contributed to a sense of not only physical but spiritual well-being. I sincerely doubt that such an experience could be had by an immaterial soul entombed in a body. If body and soul were really separate, material things could not effect the innermost parts of us in such subtle and delightful ways.

The last of my blunted tools is the word "love," and I doubt that there is a more abused word in the English language. Sometimes the word "love" appears in the titles of popular songs which are really about exploiting sexual partners. "Love" is what the blithe marketeers tell me I should feel for the car I drive or the peanut butter I eat for lunch. Others assure me that I will be "loved" if I work compliantly, shop conspicuously, and claim that being able to do so makes me free. Yet this is not what the authors of the New Testament had in mind when they used the Greek word *agape*. *Agape* is the delight God takes in his creation and the wonder that creation returns to God. It is something that goes deeper than thought, emotions, or the structures and economic arrangements of our communities. *Agape* is both the mode and product of humanity's union with God, and, when silence visits us at prayer, it is *agape* that we find flashing and shimmering within it.

So now it will mean something when I say it: at its deepest level, prayer consists in loving God with one's heart, mind, and soul. The soul is that mysterious inner power which causes us to be alive, the mind is the source of attention and action, and the heart is the center of our bodily natures. When the Holy Spirit prompts us to pray deeply, the most essential features of our corporeality, our powers of awareness, and our status of living things will be caught up

in wonder and reciprocal delight. This wonder and reciprocal delight is divine love, *agape*, and through this love we
both become one with God and even more ourselves.

Varieties of Contemplation

So far, I have been treating contemplation as though it
were a uniform experience. Most likely it is not. I suspect
that "contemplation" refers to a set of experiences in which
the divine presence grasps and to a greater or lesser extent
stills the deeper levels of the personality. A friend of mine
who was raised in the Nazarene church recounts this experience. When he was a boy, his family would attend
Wednesday evening prayer meetings. After a brief sermon,
everyone would kneel down facing the back of the church
with his or her hands resting on the seat of a pew. Then
those assembled would pray out loud, and the church would
be filled with a holy muttering. My friend says he felt the
spoken prayers wrapping around him like a warm quilt, and
even his own voice faded into the background as his awareness meandered off on its own to commune with God. I suspect that some of my older Roman Catholic friends miss the
Latin liturgy for similar reasons. The dead language made it
impossible to pay attention to what was going on in the service. Instead, the corpulent Latin vowels floated them off
on their own adventures with God.

William Law, an eighteenth century Anglican priest,
found his way into a full and rich stillness in which physical
change ceased, and God timelessly illumined all reality.
Grasping for metaphors to communicate something of the
experience to others, Law drew on Revelation 4.1–8 and
what passed for organismic biology in the 1750s:

There is no sort of strife, wrath, or storm in outward nature, no fermentation, vegetation, or corruption in any elementary things but what is a full proof and real effect of this truth, viz., that nature can have no rest but must be in the strife of fermentation, vegetation, and corruption, constantly doing and undoing, building and destroying, till the spirit of love has rectified all outward nature and brought it back into that glassy sea of unity and purity in which St. John beheld the throne of God in the midst of it. For this glassy sea, which the beloved Apostle was blessed with the sight of, is the transparent, heavenly element in which all the properties and powers move and work in the unity and purity of the one will of God, only known as so many endless forms of triumphing light and love.[2]

The science is dodgy at best, but Law's metaphor is still valid. In some experiences of contemplative prayer one senses a stillness amid the abundance of creation, and one glimpses God at the center of things gently tugging it all back toward himself. For some, contemplative prayer involves a sense of being part of a fine, glassy sea flowing silently back to God.

Quite frequently, I have contemplative experiences when I am off alone in the mountains. One summer day I found myself in a grove of aspen trees. My heart was thumping, and I tasted salt on my upper lip. The aspen leaves, dark green against white bark, rustled in a light wind, and the sky was a vivid blue. The previous night's rain left the air moist and clean. Underlying the natural beauty, I sensed the profound stillness of God's sustaining presence. I prayed by

2. William Law, *The Spirit of Love*, ed. Paul G. Stanwood (New York: Paulist Press, 1978), 363–364.

enjoying the stillness, because many words would ruin something that was, in itself, lovely and complete. It was best to let it be and to let myself be caught up in it.

Some people are fortunate enough to find themselves from time to time caught up in a lovely quiet deeper than words and mental images no matter where they are. On a bus, preparing a meal, or even in the midst of the day's work, they find themselves folded into a delightful silence that seems to encompass all the peripheral noise. Once they experience this inner silence, the words and images of mental prayer become a distraction. The thinking and imagining mind no longer seems adequate to penetrate to the real heart of things. Now they sense God dwelling at the very center of their personalities, in a region of the soul deeper even than the capacities for language, sensation, or emotion. Now they glimpse the divine presence through attentive, wonder-infused love. Whether grading papers, working in a garden, or making love, such people sense that all their actions flow out of a basic, creative stillness.

Something Is Afoot

Meister Eckhart, a thirteenth-century German mystic, liked to say that one meets God where one parts from things. He did not mean that we should become angels rather than be human beings. Rather, Eckhart wanted to emphasize that our usual ways of perceiving and knowing were inadequate for glimpsing God as he really is, and that we should quit trying to approach God as though he were just another physical or mental object. Eckhart urged his listeners to pay attention for a while to God only. Yet Eckhart could not describe what his listeners might find once they averted their attention from the domains of thought and imagination. A description would require language, something inadequate for the job and already tossed aside. Nevertheless, Eckhart stressed that one makes genuine discoveries upon entering this silence.

> But now, perhaps you say: 'What can God do in the core and essence [of the soul] without ideas?' I couldn't possibly know, for the agents of the soul deal only in ideas, taking things and naming them, each according to its own idea. . . . Since the soul itself does not know, it wonders and, wondering, it seeks, for the soul knows very well that something is afoot, even though it does not know how or what.[3]

God is afoot in the silence and unknowing of contemplative prayer, and now we have the opportunity to meet him on his own terms.

At the beginning of this chapter, I wrote about roller coaster cars poised at the top of a hill and of the delightful expectation one feels as the ride begins. Perched at the top of the first hill, one senses something is afoot although one has no immediate perception of it. When I find my way into the silence of contemplative prayer, I experience a similar but more subtle anticipation. In both experiences I sense that something is afoot within the stillness. Contemplative anticipation is special because it is not so much a fleeting moment as it is a fleeting glimpse of eternity. Ordinary clock time is no longer important. Instead, one enters the time of

---

3. Meister Eckhart, "This is Meister Eckhart from Whom God Hid Nothing," in *Meister Eckhart: A Modern Translation*, trans. Raymond Blakney (New York: Harper, 1941), 100.

opportunities. When engaged in pure loving attentiveness to God, clock time speeds by while the silence remains clear and unaltered.

So much for my trying to describe or mark the boundaries of what counts as contemplative prayer. In fact, the experience extends much deeper into us than can be reached with words or images, and so trying to *say* something sensible about it is about as effective as trying to tighten a nut with a ball peen hammer. Trying to use words to discuss something which is essentially wordless and beyond mental pictures finally turns out to be a futile exercise. In the end, I can only say that contemplation is a distinct experience, and that when the prayer of silence comes, it will be much as one expected.

Infused Contemplation

Several decades ago, those who taught and wrote about contemplative prayer went round and round about whether the prayer of quiet was "infused" or "acquired." Those favoring acquired contemplation held that it was proper to use certain techniques to enter into, or acquire, a state of holy silence, but more about this in a moment. On the other hand, those favoring infused contemplation preferred to talk about God's grace entering the soul and stilling superficial layers of consciousness. At least among Roman Catholics, this has been the dominant position from the era of the Church Fathers until fairly recently. According to the infusion theorist, the soul is something like a teapot filled with hot water; a loaded tea ball has to be dropped into the pot for the water to become tea, and, similarly, the grace of contemplation must be infused into the soul if it is to enjoy the prayer of silence. Quite properly, they pointed out that union with God is something that transpires by grace rather than human merit, and that contemplative prayer, like all other types of prayer, is a response to God's presence.

In theory, infusion was a very attractive position. In the first place, if one found oneself engaging in contemplative prayer, one could be absolutely certain that God was at work in one's soul. Since it was stipulated that contemplation was something introduced into the soul from the outside, it followed that it was not something that one initiated for oneself. Moreover, the infusion theory emphasized the gratuitousness of divine grace. Since God draws us to himself when and how he wishes, it did not seem fitting that contemplation, presumably a higher-order form of prayer, could be switched on by merely human whims. The practical consequence of the theory, however, was that friends of infused contemplation thought it presumptuous actively to seek the prayer of quiet, and so few ever experienced it.

Given that contemplation is the highest form of prayer and given that it is a gift bestowed by God as he pleases, infusion theorists reasoned that it was best to wait for God to still the soul when and how he thought best. Nonetheless, they thought that one could predispose oneself to receive the grace of contemplation, and so they placed great emphasis on those phases of the mystical journey leading up to contemplative prayer. It is not uncommon, for example, to find a champion of infused contemplation urging one to return to the ardor of conversion or to ginger up one's soul with a bit more active purgation. By continually returning to the experience of conversion, it was thought that one could pick up sufficient spiritual momentum to seek out and eradicate sins and sinful inclinations buried deep in one's personality. In this way, the joy of conversion motivated the work of active purgation. Contemplation was not to be expected until the purgative process was well under way.

An unintended consequence of this emphasis on conversion and purgation was that it led to a caste system among believers. Those with ecclesiastical positions or sufficient leisure time could devote themselves to fairly rigorous programs of spiritual development, while those busy with the concerns of day-to-day life had to reconcile themselves to a less intimate communion with God. Contemplative prayer became the bailiwick of specialists, something typically found among monks and nuns but rarely among the general population. The result was a net loss in the numbers of people having (or admitting to) contemplative experiences. The Protestant reformers exacerbated the loss of contemplative prayer among Christians when they began dismantling convents and monasteries. True, the caste system was eliminated, thank goodness, but in doing so the Reformers lost touch with Christianity's ancient, contemplative tradition. In this way, prayer with words came to occupy a preeminent place in Protestant spirituality.

On the other side of the ideological divide, Roman Catholics responded by circling their theological wagons. Not knowing when private experience might shake loose another Luther or Calvin, the Roman Catholics tucked their contemplatives further away and saw to it that abbots and father confessors ride herd on the mystics. To be taken seriously, the mystic now had to prove that he or she was in earnest, and the approved way of doing so was to put up with whatever one's superiors did to one. What emerged was a cult of suffering. Put in the double bind of either denying one's experience or being baited because of it, contemplatives came to see the journey into the heart of God as coextensive with the Way of the Cross. This is a sad aberration, and no more needs be said of it.

Acquired Contemplation

Although the theory of infused contemplation was for centuries the dominant approach to the prayer of quiet in the Western Church, it was never the only one. Among Eastern Orthodox Christians, a tradition of acquired contemplation called *hesychasm* (from the modern Greek word for stillness or fixedness) dates back to at least the eighth century. An engaging introduction to *hesychasm* can be found in a small eighteenth century work called *The Way of a Pilgrim*. An older and more detailed approach can be found in the multi-volume *Philokalia*. In fourteenth century England, an anonymous country pastor described a way of acquired contemplation in a delightful little book called *The Cloud of Unknowing*. This late medieval work forms the basis for a contemporary practice called centering prayer developed by Trappist priest William Meninger and popularized by other members of his order. Even Saint Teresa of Avila, a sixteenth century mystic usually associated with the theory of infused contemplation, provides some instruction in the art of acquired contemplation in one of her books, *The Interior Castle*.

Presently, I will discuss the methods of Saint Teresa, the hesychasts, and *The Cloud of Unknowing*. Before launching that practical discussion, I would like to take a moment to tie up just one loose end. As we noticed earlier, the chief virtue of the theory of infused contemplation was that it emphasized divine grace rather than human ingenuity. This led friends of infused contemplation to regard contemplative prayer as a gift that one did not seek but, rather, something for which one prepared oneself. Unfortunately, this way of seeing things sometimes led to the view that the practice of acquired contemplation was an uppity attempt to hurry grace. I suppose that some people who practiced various forms of acquired contemplation have behaved badly after forgetting that all prayer is a response to God's grace. However, this is not a problem unique to the practice of acquired contemplation. Any spiritual practice turns rotten when used as a way of compelling God to do things for us. In these instances, magical thinking preempts genuine faith.

Typically, the practice of acquired contemplation begins with one's desire for a more intimate communion with God. Insofar as it is genuine, and it would be highly unusual if it were not, such a desire is the product of God's grace. Consequently, the very act of taking up the practice of acquired contemplation is itself a response to grace. As Saint Augustine says, God created us for himself, and our hearts are not quiet until they rest in him.[4] The Creator is at work even in our hopes and desires, and if we feel the desire to pray it is reasonable to assume that it is present because God placed it in us. Consequently, the desire of contemplation is not normally a mark of vainglory, but rather evidence that our true nature is beginning to surface.

---

4. Augustine, *Confessions* I.1.

Some Methods of Contemplative Prayer

To begin the practice of contemplation, find a quiet place where you will not be disturbed, and plan on visiting it for a half hour each day. A spare room, a park, or even a neglected corner of a library will do. Each time you come to that place, remember that you have come to meet God there and that anything less will not be satisfactory. Make sure that you are comfortable, but if you keep your back straight and both feet on the floor you will be less likely to drop off to sleep. If you close your eyes or focus them about three feet in front of you, you will be less likely to be distracted. To keep track of time, ask someone to knock on your door after a half hour or set an alarm clock. I have been told that one can buy sticks of incense that will burn for about half an hour, and so this is another option. As you progress in the practice of contemplation, it will become less and less necessary to observe these rules of thumb.

Saint Teresa of Avila advised nuns under her direction to begin seeking contemplation by saying the Lord's Prayer. Teresa instructed her nuns to say the prayer's words slowly to themselves without wagging either lips or tongues. To slow the portion of the mind which traffics in words and images even further, Teresa suggested that the interior words be synchronized with one's breathing. For example, one might breath in while repeating the word "our" and out when saying the word "Father." Upon reaching the end of the prayer one simply begins again and continues until the time for prayer has ended. If one finds one's mind wandering, one merely returns to reciting the prayer.

There is no hoodoo involved in Teresa's breathing exercises. She believed that one should be relaxed but attentive while praying and that one's manner of breathing should reflect this. When someone falls asleep, the belly rises as the person inhales and falls as he or she exhales. This is because the diaphragm is drawing air deep into the lungs. In a waking state this kind of breathing brings both relaxation and mental clarity. It is with this supple clarity that one approaches the divine presence and waits there loving God with one's whole heart, mind, and soul.

After performing Saint Teresa's exercise for a while, one's mind might begin to wander. One might find oneself thinking about the theory of contemplation rather than doing it, reliving a recent squabble, or wondering what to fix for supper. In such cases, the discursive intellect thrusts itself to the forefront of consciousness, and our more subtle awareness of holy silence scuttles away like an Indian villager fleeing a rogue elephant. Now there are several ways to tranquilize the elephant. In some instances, it might be sufficient to pay a bit more attention to the words of the Lord's Prayer which one is already saying. This may well provide the discursive intellect with enough fodder so that it will no longer be a nuisance. If words, images, and emotions are still stamping around in one's head, one may also try leaving them there and shifting the focus of attention to the pit of one's stomach or elsewhere in the body. When all else fails, it is time to mock the elephant. Notice the relative banality of the nuisance thoughts and resolve not to allow them to pry one's gaze away from God's presence. At this point, the elephant will probably become tired of playing with one and lumber off to the periphery of consciousness.

What hesychasts call "the Prayer of the Heart" is similar to Saint Teresa's way of saying the Lord's Prayer, but it involves fewer words. Rather than the entire Lord's Prayer, the Prayer of the Heart consists of a single sentence: "Lord Jesus Christ, Son of the Living God, / have mercy upon me a sinner," an adaptation of the publican's prayer in Luke 18.9–14. While breathing in, one invokes Jesus's name remembering that God desires to bring us back to the divine likeness through the incarnation. While breathing out, one imagines expelling from oneself all that is not of God and then begins again. After a while, the prayer becomes simpler, and one may find oneself saying simply "Jesus" or "mercy." Having become comfortable saying the prayer in this way, one becomes aware of one's heartbeat. While continuing to repeat the words of the prayer to oneself, one synchronizes the words or syllables to the beating of one's heart.

There is a great deal of theological sophistication packed into this little prayer. First, it invokes image-to-likeness theology within the context of the Incarnation. By becoming a human being, Christ ennobled humanity by restoring in himself our lost likeness to God. In this sense, Jesus *is* as we hope to be (see Hebrews 10.19–23; Romans 5.12–21; Philippians 2.6–11). The Prayer of the Heart dramatizes the journey back to the divine likeness. While breathing in we fill ourselves with the nobility of the Incarnation, and in breathing out we expel what has become noisome within us. Second, the Prayer of the Heart is a very explicit way of loving God with one's whole heart, soul, and mind. The heart, the center of one's physical being, literally beats with the words of the prayer, and in this way enables the mind to direct its full attention to the love of God. In this way, the whole person stands attentively before God seeking to recover his or her lost likeness through Christ.

The way of contemplative prayer recommended in *The Cloud of Unknowing* involves even fewer words than the

Prayer of the Heart. In this instance, one chooses a single, preferably one-syllable, word such as "God" or "love" and gently repeats it whenever the discursive intellect gets rambunctious and needs to be quieted. God is afoot, as it were, above one hidden by a "cloud of unknowing," and one stuffs all words and images beneath one in a "cloud of forgetting." To borrow a phrase from a friend of mine, it is a methodless method. Its essence consists in seeking God through a loving stillness and in maintaining one's attention to the divine presence through the discrete use of the single word. Eventually, one tosses even the word aside and is aware of divine stillness only.

Finally, it is worth repeating here that the silence one seeks is not that of emptiness or resignation, but rather the small, still voice of God (see 1 Kings 19.11–13). The silence and seeming nothingness is the result of the inadequacies of our perceptual and intellectual equipment; these faculties cannot grasp God as he is. But we can love as God loves, and in this way God joins us to him. Although our loving can take on the same quality as God's love, it can never be as far-reaching or as potent. Although we may, so to speak, sound the same note as God, we will never do so as beautifully or as intensely. In this way we become one with God without becoming the same entity as God. Contemplative prayer is the art of such union.

Chapter 6

⌘

The Winter Journey

*This is very strange that God should want. For in him is the
fullness of all Blessedness: He overflowed eternally. His wants
are as glorious as infinite: perfective needs are in His nature and
ever Blessed, because always satisfied. He is from eternity full
of want, or else He would not be full of treasure. Infinite want
is the very ground and cause of infinite treasure. It is incredible,
yet very plain. Want is the foundation of all his His fullness*
— Thomas Traherne, *Centuries*, I.42

Whence, Then, Is Evil?

A few years ago I taught on a campus that received
bomb threats. A poster explaining how to spot letter and
package bombs hung in the room where I had my mail box.
One afternoon in early autumn as an overcast sky spat the
first snow of the season my students told me that the science building had been evacuated and that news of a bomb
threat was all over the local radio stations. When I finished my lecture I found a pay phone and called Barbara
seventy miles away in Golden. Barbara had not heard
about the bomb scare—which by this time had turned out
to be only a scare—but she did tell me that a hard snow
had begun and that she had covered as many of the plants

119

in our garden as she could. Perhaps a handful of tomato plants and melons could be salvaged and ripen over the next two weeks.

I drove home with snowflakes whirling in the headlights and arrived in Golden around eleven. I made a point to come into my neighborhood along Washington Avenue, our main street, and the Victorian houses and store fronts I had known from my boyhood assured me that I was home. Soon Barbara and I were in bed and asleep. Around ten the next morning the snow had melted, and I went out into the garden to survey the damage. Except for a few cabbages and pea vines, anything left uncovered was withered and greenish-black. Summer was over, and suddenly I felt a weight of things lost or wasted which extended far beyond the garden's boundaries.

As one continues on the journey into the divine likeness, suffering, cruelty, and waste must be confronted more than once. I have not yet heard an adequate explanation of why it is that one suffers in body or mind or is pained to see the pain of others. A Greek philosopher named Epicurus (341–270 BCE) once asked:

> Is [God] willing to prevent evil, but unable to do so? Then he is impotent. Is he able but unwilling? Then [God] is malevolent. Is he both willing and able? Whence, then, is evil?

On the face of it, Epicurus's questions remain unanswered, and it seems almost indecent to attempt to furnish any. There are, I suppose, few sentences more noisome than those beginning with the words, "You're suffering because. . . ."

Recall some recent and senseless tragedy, there are always many among which one may choose, and then imagine explaining to someone on the receiving end of it why God allowed it to happen. There are two general strategies. On one hand, one might take the brazen approach and tell the person suffering that she is in pain now to pay for past mistakes. It makes no difference to say that the victim herself made the mistake in this life, or some past life. In either case, one blames the victim, and I doubt that this is either helpful or particularly sporting. If these fail, one might tell her that her pain comes as the result of some connection to the mistakes of her forebears and that she has inherited the responsibility for their mistakes. Once again, the advice is not especially fetching; the victim must suffer to pay off a debt which she never chose to incur. On the other hand, one may go in for cockeyed optimism and claim that the senseless tragedy is not really senseless at all, but an opportunity for her to build her character. In this case our friend might rightly reply that she never asked to have her character built and urge us not to let the door whack our back sides on the way out.

The Dark Night of the Soul

This chapter will try to get at the problem of pain from the inside by examining an aspect of the journey into the divine likeness traditionally called the dark night of the soul. As such, what I will say here is addressed to those who already believe; at best, all a nonbeliever can expect from me is logical consistency. In other words, what I will say about pain is compatible with faith in God but not a substitute for faith. The dark night is an intensely painful experience. Slightly more advanced seekers of the divine likeness enter into it once they begin questioning the value of the

journey they have undertaken. The night may be characterized by doubts about God's love for one, doubts about God's
goodness, or, more common among people of the late twentieth century, doubts about God's existence. Yet those who
have experienced the night commonly look back on it and
find a particularly vivid instance of God's presence at the
epicenter of their doubts and worries. They see it, of course,
with the eyes of faith, but some realities can only be discerned in this way.

By embarking upon the purgative way, the newly-
converted attempt to prepare themselves for deeper communion with God by developing habits which make it easier
to cooperate with God's grace and by honing those aspects
of themselves which have so far impeded such cooperation.
In the purgative way the focus is always on becoming fit for
the journey, not on the journey itself or one's motives for
undertaking it. The dark night is a new and deeper sort of
purification. The dark night does not pertain to the habits
and dispositions of the effective pilgrim but, rather, one's
basic understanding of the pilgrimage and one's central
motivations for undertaking it.

Often the night begins subtly. The illuminative way, as
we have seen, is marked by a vivid sense of one's connection
to God and God's creation. As the illuminative way progresses, mystics often experience interruptions in their sense
of connectedness, and the feeling of God's absence may last
for a few hours or a few days. Often one's sense of God's
absence will be accompanied not so much by unease as boredom. While previously church services and private prayer
served to intensify one's feelings of love and gratitude
toward God, now these activities seem tedious. What was
delightful and engaging now becomes a duty to be dis-

charged or avoided altogether. Prayer becomes as dry as a lecture on German grammar. Among those on the illuminative way these periodic episodes of spiritual aridity may continue for several years or even seem like a game of spiritual hide-and-seek. But then one day one looks in all the usual hiding places and finds nothing. A door closes, a key is lost, and one is thrown back upon one's own resources. So begins the dark night of the soul.

The onset of the dark night may or may not coincide with an upheaval in the external circumstances of one's life. The dark night may be preceded by nothing more than unemphatic slippage from the lights and pleasures of the illuminative way, or the door may shut abruptly. I have chosen three instances of the dark night, all involving emphatic and abrupt changes in the subject's life. I have done so because it is easier to follow the night's progress in such cases. While others may have experienced the night in a more nondescript form, this does not mean that their nights were less genuine.

Before turning to these cases, however, I should make a few remarks about the duration of the night and how it is identified. First, according to the classical authorities, the dark night lasts for about two years. My friends who have experienced the dark night also tell me that their experiences lasted for between one and three years. For these reasons, I assume that figures such as Thérèse of Lisieux (fl. 1890) and Paul of the Cross (fl. 1760) who report substantially longer nights are exceptions rather than representatives of a general pattern of mystical experience. Second, those who have experienced the dark night recognize it most clearly in hindsight. Having experienced a string of shocks and misfortunes and having been transformed by dealing with them in a forthright manner, God's grace may permit one to look back on the ordeal and discover a coherent pattern in it. While someone is in the midst of the night, he or she will not have the perspective to discern its overall structure. The dark night is not fully known until it has been lived fully.

(1) Dmitri Shostakovich: Hero of Socialist Labor

The Russian composer Dmitri Shostakovich (1906–1975) never practiced the Christian faith. Nevertheless, there is something of the divine in everyone's creative powers. Shostakovich's fidelity to his substantial gifts brought him into contact with many facets of the dark night, and this makes his story a good place to begin. Shostakovich completed his First Symphony when he was nineteen years old, and after its 1926 premier he was well on his way to an international reputation. By 1930 both Auturo Toscanini and Leopold Stowski had included the piece in their repertoires, and fashionable opinion had it that Shostakovich would be the twentieth century successor to Tschaikowsky and Mussorgsky. Yet rather than writing music in the style of nineteenth century Russian romantics, Shostakovich experimented with complex rhythms and chose to construct works based on the interplay of tonal colorations rather than simple melodies.

Shostakovich's compositions were new, witty, and, for a while, successful. Photographs of this period show an introverted young man with thin lips and thick glasses seemingly well aware of the scope of his gifts. Then in 1936 Shostakovich's ordeal began. Shostakovich's second opera *Lady Macbeth of the Mtsensk District* had recently opened and had been received favorably until the night Joseph Stalin appeared in the audience. The lights dimmed, Shostakovich's music filled the hall, and halfway through the performance Stalin stamped out of the theatre. The next day an unsigned editorial, "Muddle Instead of Music," appeared in *Pravda.* Stalin himself had dictated it.

Lady Macbeth of the Mtsensk District promptly closed, the premiere of Shostakovich's Fourth Symphony was cancelled, and for the next seventeen years Shostakovich would live in fear of Stalin. In 1937 the KGB executed Shostakovich's chief patron, and Shostakovich himself had good reason to fear death or internal exile. Thirty-five years later, Shostakovich would write, "Awaiting execution is a theme that has tormented me all my life. Many pages of my music are devoted to it."[1] Now Shostakovich was expected to produce music that would please Stalin and his commissars. He survived by writing scores for movies and subtitled his Fifth Symphony, "A Soviet Artist's Reply to Just Criticism." Meanwhile, Shostakovich kept his thoughts to himself and continued with his own projects in his spare time. If he thought one of these compositions would fail to please, he slipped it into the bottom drawer of his desk with the hope that someday it would be performed.

Shostakovich recognized that the ultimate significance of his life was bound up with the practice of his art, and that his unique talents would be wasted were he to be exiled or executed. He chose to endure, and over the years became an inside-outside figure in the world of Soviet fine arts. On one hand, even Stalin recognized that Shostakovich was a

---

1. Dmitri Shostakovich, *Testimony*, ed. Solmon Volkov (New York: Limelight Editions, 1979), 183.

genius with an international reputation to be taken into account. When he was not busy castigating him Stalin saw to it that Shostakovich received all the prestigious awards that the Soviet state could give its artists. On the other hand, Stalin and his successors treated Shostakovich as a commodity to be exploited. Shostakovich was obliged to read speeches prepared by his keepers, and he did so in a quiet monotone. Articles under his name appeared in *Pravda* even though Shostakovich had neither written nor even seen them. Shostakovich occasionally traveled abroad as an official representative of the Soviet Union, but his wife and children did not accompany him. The authorities feared that he would defect.

In 1960, Shostakovich had the misfortune of being appointed first secretary of the Russian composer's union. This meant that he would have to join the Communist party for the first time and give a grateful speech for having had the opportunity to do so. As usual, the authorities had drafted the speech, and Shostakovich read along in his usual monotone never raising his eyes from the paper. Then the composer raised his voice unexpectedly, lifted his eyes from the paper, and said in a clear, loud voice, "For everything good about me I am indebted to. . . ." The audience expected to hear the mandatory tribute to the Soviet government and Communist party. Instead, Shostakovich concluded, "my parents!"

In the years between Stalin's visit to the theatre in 1937 and Shostakovich's death in 1975 he composed ten more symphonies, fifteen string quartets, several concertos and choral works, and was named a Hero of Socialist Labor. Shostakovich was faithful to his gift and at a great psychic cost produced a body of work equal in scope, quantity, and quality to that of Mozart. Despite his energy and integrity,

Shostakovich remained a trapped genius, and this fact infused his life with a grey bitterness. Toward the end of his life Shostakovich wrote:

> I have thought that my life was replete with sorrow and that it would be hard to find a more miserable man. But when I started going over the life stories of my friends and acquaintances, I was horrified. Not one of them had an easy or a happy life. Some came to a terrible end, some died in terrible suffering, and the lives of many of them could be called more miserable than mine. And that made me even sadder.[2]

We hear the sadness in his music, but we also hear something of the integrity of a man who soldiered on alone trying to be faithful to what was uniquely good within him.

(2) John Donne: All That She Does Belongs to All

In 1623 the Reverend Doctor John Donne, once a writer of love poems and now the sober dean of London's St. Paul's Cathedral, felt the first chills of a fever and went to bed. The disease progressed, and as one of Donne's contemporaries put it, the sickness "inclined him to a consumption . . . and threatened him with death."[3] It is not clear whether Donne suffered from tuberculosis, influenza, rheumatic fever, or some combination of these. Donne himself wrote

---

2. *Testimony*, 276.

3. Izaak Walton, *The Life of Dr. John Donne* excerpted in *John Donne: Devotions Upon Emergent Occasions* (Ann Arbor: University of Michigan Press, 1959), xxvi.

that his vision failed, that his limbs ached, and that he felt as though he were nailed to his bed. Donne's physicians expected that their patient would die and feared that they would become infected themselves. Neither occurred, and during a lengthy convalescence Donne composed an account of his interior struggles during his illness, *Meditations Upon Emergent Occasions*.

Donne's *Devotions* recount his inner dialogue with God as his illness progressed. When Donne first feels the fever's fingers playing up and down his backbone, he remembers that human beings are really rather fragile. A bit of a fever, and one's dinner becomes insipid. A couple more degrees, and the day's projects must be abandoned. A few more degrees, and the body is irreparably damaged. Donne takes to his bed. Years ago, when he was healthy, Donne wrote poems about long mornings spent in bed with his new wife:

> So must pure lovers' souls descend
> 　　T' affections, and to faculties,
> Which sense may reach and apprehend,
> 　　Else a great prince in prison lies.
> To' our bodies turn we then that so
> 　　Weak men on love reveal'd may look;
> Love's mysteries in souls do grow,
> 　　But yet the body is his book.[4]

Now Donne is a widower, and he discovers that he cannot rise from his bed. Friends send for a physician, but the doctor fears that Donne is contagious and delays coming.

---

4. John Donne, "The Ecstasy."

Donne himself feels abandoned. Like the doctor, his friends and family care about him, but insofar as possible they keep their distance. God seems to be an indifferent observer, not a vital presence revealed in human interaction.

A long sickness will weary friends. At last, but a pestilential sickness averts them from the beginning. God himself would admit a figure of society, as there is a plurality of persons in God, and all his external actions testify a love of society and communion. In heaven, there are orders of angels, and armies of martyrs in that house of many mansions; in earth, families, cities, churches, colleges, all plural things; and lest either of these should not be company enough alone, there is an association of both, a communion of saints which makes the militant and triumphant church one parish.[5]

But Donne is alone. Because his disease cuts him off from family and friends, Donne also feels cut off from the divine likeness. The Christian faith tells us that God is, so to speak, a perfect community, a Trinity, three persons made one through an infinite love for one another. By being isolated from family and friends, Donne feels unable to live out this aspect of the divine nature. Excluded from the warmth of human contact. Donne cannot feel at one with God.

The illness grows worse, and Donne hears someone slowly ringing a church bell to signal that a member of the parish is near death. Donne reflects that perhaps the bell is being rung for him or, perhaps, for someone who has already

---

5. *Devotions*, 30.

lapsed into unconsciousness and does not hear its sound at all. Then Donne achieves a breakthrough. For whom the bell tolls is not an either-or proposition. Each member of the parish, the sick and the well, the dead and the living are one in the mystical body of Christ.

> The church is Catholic, universal, so are all her actions; all that she does belongs to all. When she baptizes a child, that action concerns me; for the child is thereby connected to my head too, and ingrafted into that body whereof I am a member. And when she buries a man, that action concerns me. . . . [A]ny man's death diminishes me, because I am involved in mankind, and therefore never send to know for whom the bell tolls; it tolls for thee.[6]

The bell tolls for each of us because we are all implicated in one another's lives. The mystical body of Christ is no mere metaphor but, rather, a fact one discovers by transcending one's own pain by taking others' lives into account. As an Anglican hymn for All Saints Day puts it, "all are one for all are thine."

(3) C. S. Lewis: A Chuckle in the Darkness

Helen Joy Gresham died of bone cancer on July 11, 1960. She had married C. S. Lewis in her hospital room three and a half years earlier. Lewis was fifty-eight years old then and had been a lifelong bachelor before the marriage. Joy was in her early forties, divorced, with two sons. The couple seized the time allowed by a remission of her cancer and worked to

---

6. *Devotions, 107–109.*

stuff all the depth and intensity of a lifelong partnership into what both knew would be a much shorter time. Lewis alluded to those three and a half years in *A Grief Observed*, his journal of the weeks following Joy's death:

> For those few years H. and I feasted on love; every mode of it—solemn and merry, romantic and realistic, sometimes as dramatic as a thunderstorm, sometimes as comfortable and unemphatic as putting on your slippers. No cranny of heart or body remained unsatisfied.[7]

More than this, Lewis's marriage drew him out of the cozy but hidebound world of an academic bachelor and into "something very close and intimate yet all the time unmistakably other, resistant—in a word, real."[8]

But in the summer of 1960 Lewis was alone again. He was alarmed that he could not picture Joy's face and worried that his memory of her would devolve into something little better than a bachelor's pipe-dream. Lewis feared that he would not remember his wife as she was but as he would have liked her to be, and he worried that he would slip again into comfortable, insular, academic bachelorhood. "Oh God, God," he wrote, "why did you take such trouble to force this creature out of its shell if now it is doomed to crawl back—to be sucked back—into it?"[9] The problem was one of waste. Lewis believed that his falling in love with Joy was a providential event that showed him more about God's love than

---

7. C. S. Lewis, *A Grief Observed* (San Francisco: HarperCollins, 1961), 23–24.

8. *A Grief Observed*, 34–35.

9. *A Grief Observed*, 35.

decades of solitary reflection. Now he was being forced to return to that solitude. Lewis's journey of discovery and wonder was terminated, and the pain that replaced it served no positive purpose.

Years earlier, he had an answer. In *The Problem of Pain* Lewis asserted that "God whispers to us in our pleasures, speaks in our conscience, but shouts in our pains: it is his megaphone to rouse a deaf world."[10] Lewis had argued that God allows us to experience pain in order to discipline our rebellious souls. Pain exists to shock us out of self-absorption and our illusion of self-sufficiency, and, said Lewis, all are in need of the treatment because all are sinners.

> The creature's illusion of self-sufficiency must, for the creature's sake, be shattered; and by trouble or fear of trouble on earth, by crude fear of eternal flames, God shatters it 'unmindful of His glory's diminution.'[11]

In *The Problem of Pain* God emerges as a figure much like a Victorian headmaster who confronts his charges with the results of their behavior and awaits a properly docile response.

In the summer of 1960, however, Lewis had become a walking counterexample to his earlier opinions. His love for Joy, not a dose of corrective pain, had drawn him out of his complacent shell, and the pain of her loss threatened to drive him back into himself. God had shouted in Lewis's love for Joy, and he could not discern even a whisper of God's goodness in the pain he felt when she died.

---

10. C. S. Lewis, *The Problem of Pain* (London: Collins, 1940), 81.
11. *The Problem of Pain*, 85.

No, my real fear is not of materialism. If it were true, we . . . could get out, get from under the harrow. An overdose of sleeping pills would do it. I am more afraid that we are really rats in a trap. Or, worse still, rats in a laboratory. Someone said, I believe, 'God always geometrizes.' Supposing the truth were 'God always vivisects'?[12]

Suppose that God were not a benevolent school master dispensing pains like vitamins but, rather, a malevolent force that delights in raising our hopes only to frustrate them. Lewis noted that God was capable both of creating Beethoven and of allowing him to go deaf. Had God brought C. S. Lewis and Joy Gresham together not to instruct them through their love but to thwart and cancel whatever goodness their love produced?

The problem lay in Lewis's notion of a God who used pain as a megaphone. While it is not beyond God's power to draw good out of evil by using pain to awaken someone from self-absorption, this is not enough to justify each and every painful experience. Lewis's grieving over Joy was one such case. When we view pain exclusively as God's megaphone, we implicitly assume that someone, somewhere must accept the blame for its presence. Lewis knew that he was not responsible for Joy's death and that his sorrow because of it was what any sane person might expect to feel. Lewis was certain that his pain arose from his love of Joy, and it would be indecent to repent of *that*. If pain was a megaphone, then it made perfect sense to question the motives of the being wielding it.

The resolution of the problem of pain in *A Grief Observed* closely parallels the resolution of Lewis's worries about his

---

12. *A Grief Observed*, 46.

inability to hold on to an accurate mental image of Joy. A photograph or memory of someone we love is not the same thing as the person, and to believe otherwise is to make a representation of the thing loved into a graven image. As Lewis put it: "I want H., not something that is like her. A really good photograph might become in the end a snare, a horror, and an obstacle."[13] Images, whether in the mind or on paper are merely links to a person. Lewis realized that he loved Joy, not the idea of her. Similarly, Lewis recognized that his image of God as a megaphone-wielding schoolmaster was merely an image, not God himself.

> Images of the Holy easily become holy images—sacrosanct. My idea of God is not a divine idea. It has to be shattered time after time. He shatters it Himself. He is the great iconoclast. Could we not almost say that this shattering is one of the marks of his presence?[14]

Of course, none of this solves the problem of pain. However, Lewis's new way of seeing things did remove some self-imposed barriers.

By choosing not to cling to images of Joy, Lewis began to feel closer to her. Part of love is a readiness to be surprised and a willingness to set aside preconceptions. Lewis chose to continue loving, and the choice itself allowed for a new range of possibilities.

> One moment last night can be described in similes; otherwise it won't go into language at all. Imagine a man in total

---

13. *A Grief Observed*, 83.
14. *A Grief Observed*, 83.

darkness. He thinks he is in a cellar or dungeon. Then there comes a sound. He thinks it might be a sound from far off—waves or wind-blown trees or cattle half a mile away. And if so, it proves he's not in a cellar, but free in the open air. Or it may be a much smaller sound close at hand—a chuckle of laughter. And if so, there is a friend beside him in the dark. Either way, a good, good sound.[15]

Love, Lewis discovered, is a way of knowing, but what is known are not the answers but the beloved.

God's Work

When Christ encounters pain in the Gospels, he does not try to figure out who is to blame for it. He heals it. The problem of assigning responsibility for suffering obsesses those who surround him, but it never occurs to Christ himself.

> As he walked along, he saw a man blind from birth. His disciples asked him, "Rabbi, who sinned, this man or his parents, that he was born blind?" Jesus answered, "Neither this man nor his parents sinned; he was born blind so that God's works might be revealed in him." (John 9.1–3)

Human beings know God chiefly as the creator and sustainer of the universe. All the truths of revealed religion point back toward this one fact. Christ became incarnate to draw creation back to the Father through himself, and the Father sent the Holy Spirit to infuse creation with divine love. God's work as creator consists in drawing what exists

---

15. *A Grief Observed*, 81.

from what does not exist, in sustaining what does exist, and in drawing what is good from good's absence.

Christ immediately identifies both himself and his disciples with the Father's activity: "We must work the works of him who sent me" (John 9.4). Then he cures the blind man. For the Christian, the problem of evil is answered not by an indicative sentence but by an imperative. There is evil in the world because God's work is not finished. Christ calls us not to help him inventory sins but to share in the creative work of God himself. We must work the works and not waste time counting up what is lacking. A friend once told me that he thought that humans were never banished from the Garden of Eden but, rather, chose no longer to cultivate it.

My friend was speaking in the language of metaphor. He meant that God created us like himself and that in coming round again to who we truly are, we come to share in the divine project of loving, sustaining, and completing what God has begun in us and in everything that surrounds us. To live in the divine image and grow into the divine likeness means becoming one with God. But this does not mean that we are doomed to be absorbed and finished off by a power grander than ourselves. It means that we are capable of an active love qualitatively identical to God's. In a symphony orchestra the oboe and a double bass can play the same note. Their sounds will combine into a chord sounding through the rest of the orchestra, and the chords will succeed one another forming a piece first heard only in the mind of the composer. Similarly, you, I, and all that surrounds us may combine to bring forth what God has intended all along.

In fact, there are some tunes which only an individual can play. Hard-won integrity, concern for the lives of others, and love which sets the beloved free are among them. In their pain, Shostakovich, Donne, and Lewis (to use an old but satisfactory word) begat in themselves, respectively, integrity, universal compassion, and a love which does not cling to the shadows cast by things. These are things God desperately wants loosed upon the world, but they are things that God cannot instigate without doing violence to his image in us. Some things are by nature unreal, for example, a round cube or a pastry chef who is simultaneously fat and skinny. To be a creature made in God's likeness means, in part, being able to initiate acts of integrity, regard for others, or love. To be real, to be true bearers of the divine likeness, means to be able to stand on our own two feet. God cannot compel bravery, love, or a change of heart without changing a human being into a machine, something incapable of joining in the work of its creator or, metaphorically, of walking with God in a garden in the cool of the day (see Genesis 3.8). To be a bearer of God's likeness means being a bearer of his creative power. If this is to mean anything, then we must live in a world that is not yet complete, that is, imperfect.

God Afoot, God Alone, God Himself

Once when I was in Houston I visited the Rothko Chapel on the campus of the University of St. Thomas. The Rothko Chapel is a sparse, windowless, brick octagon about fifty feet wide completed in 1970. After passing through a foyer and being asked to observe silence, the visitor enters a space paved with grey cobblestones and lit by a skylight. Mark Rothko's fifteen-foot paintings hang on each of the eight walls. At first sight, each painting looks the same, a massive black surface unbroken by color or line. After a few minutes, something else about the paintings emerges. They are not just black, and they are not the same. Standing in the center of the chapel facing forward, I felt the gathering blackness of the canvases behind and beside me, and I felt myself drawn forward. The three paintings that hung in what would have been the apse of a Byzantine church shimmered faintly with maroon, and I felt my eyes being pulled to the center of the triptych to gaze on nothing in particular. There was something of the divine in that as when the god of our preconceptions slips away, and God himself arrives.

C. S. Lewis remarked that the shattering of preconceptions is one of the marks of God's presence. If this is so, then the dark night of the soul is a particularly graced moment. In the midst of the dark night, as if on the periphery of one's vision, the divine begins to break into the ordinary activities of daily life. As the opening progresses, God's inner and enveloping presence seem woven together and woven into oneself. Yet one remains distinctly oneself, or, perhaps, one is at last oneself. The boundaries between the sacred and the profane drop, because all is, indeed, God's, and while struggles continue both in oneself and in the world at large something new appears.

Chapter 7

The Divine Likeness

*Had I been alive in Adam's stead, how should I have admired
the Glories of the world! What a confluence of Thoughts and
wonders, and joys, and thanksgivings would have replenished
me . . . in so bright a dwelling place.*
— Thomas Traherne, *Centuries*, I.65

The Mirror Maze

Our local amusement park calls its hall of mirrors the
Crystal Palace. Patrons shuffle through the Crystal Palace
with their hands stretched out in front of them. This is one
of the rules. Too many people were getting bloody noses
from walking into the plate glass. If not deadly, Crystal
Palace confusion had turned inconvenient. A hall of mirrors
traffics in two kinds of illusions: one may blink back at end-
lessly reduplicated images of oneself or wander into blind
corridors that promise but do not deliver a way out of the
maze. I do not so much like finding my way through the
Crystal Palace as stepping out of it. Stepping out onto a side-
walk a few feet from where I stepped into the hall of mirrors,
I am relieved to look at substantial objects rather than reflections of myself and to stand on a substantial cement ribbon
that leads to some real place, even if only a popcorn stand.

The transforming union, the final leg of the mystical journey, is something like stepping out of a hall of mirrors and into the plain light of common day. All the constraints, frustrations, and joys of ordinary life remain, but now one sees them again as if for the first time. We have seen that one of the defining features of Christian love, and of genuine Christianity, is its capacity for wonder and its recognition of the uniqueness of the beloved. In conversion, this delighted recognition of the beloved is not unlike being swept off one's feet in the first stage of a romance. At the end of the journey, one enjoys the almost domestic pleasure of the beloved's day-to-day presence. In the transforming union, the wonder and delight remain, but the commonplace is changed. God is now present in the ordinary things of daily life much as an old friend, and while old struggles may remain, they now appear as familiar, surmountable territory.

The nature of Christian love precludes any account of mystical union that would have God absorb or snuff out our personalities. As the letter to the Ephesians puts it, we are one with Christ as members of his mystical body (see Ephesians 4.7–16). A living body flourishes when each of its parts performs its unique function. Similarly, the communion of saints, the living and the dead together, is at its best only in its pluriformity. Just as a successful marriage or a genuine friendship preserves and even enhances the uniqueness of the partners, our recovery of the divine likeness allows us to become more, not less, ourselves.

We have seen that early on in the mystical journey those undergoing conversion are typically tantalized by the possibility that there is more to reality than what is encountered in three dimensions by the five senses. The possibilities of Christian love and the desire for the divine likeness reveal a new inner geography to the newly converted, and they quickly set out to explore it. Along the way, particularly in the dark night, they find themselves blinking back at reflections of themselves or peering down dead-end corridors where once they had thought God resided. With the help of God's grace, it is possible to pick our way through the labyrinth of the self and to trade our notions about God for an awareness of God himself. Walking the labyrinth of the self is rarely pleasant, and finally to step again into the common world where other people appear as other people and God as God comes as an immense relief.

So what is the transforming union? At its roots lies a kind of second sight, usually a hard-won capacity to behold the world as something delightful and other than oneself and to join with what is beheld through loving wonder. Several chapters ago I told the story of Saint Benedict's vision. At the end of a vigil Benedict saw the first light of dawn shining through a window. A million flecks of dust tumbled one over another in the golden light, and in this ordinary sight Benedict saw the likeness of God's care of the world. God's creative and sustaining power permeates creation in the way sunlight visits us at dawn. The light of sunrise is beautiful in itself and it brings with it all the promise of the coming day. Similarly, as the divine likeness begins to glow within us we already partake of the transforming union. Among Christians, this typically begins at baptism and deepens through a lifetime's adventures. Rather than being some special sort of creature, a Christian mystic is simply someone who seeks to live-out the promises of his or her baptism. Although some Christians may be further along in this project than the rest of us, the basic features of their journeys are just the same as our own.

Ourselves and One Another

Two promises are made at baptism: we (or our families for us if we are small) promise faithfulness on the Christian journey, and those witnessing the event promise to support us along the way. Right from the beginning, the Christian path weaves our lives into the lives of others. This was John Donne's insight as he struggled with the isolation imposed by his sickness, Antony's as he prayed alone in the desert, and of my monastic friend who went to Israel and took more pleasure in the people he met along the way than in any of the holy places. In the Episcopal *Book of Common Prayer* the Sunday intercessions often conclude with the words, "Let us commend ourselves, and one another, and all our life to Christ our God." The sense of the words runs around and through the congregation, and in that moment we have some intimation of ourselves as both one and many.

At its best, marriage allows us to experience what it is like to be both at one with another person and yet oneself. One of the first things a newly married couple learns is that they cannot be satellites of one another. It is not enough to sacrifice one's wants or needs for the sake of a spouse while expecting the spouse to return the favor. Such an arrangement may be disguised by a superficial, self-abnegating piety, but its real basis is mutual exploitation. The focus remains upon what one gives up rather than on the possibilities opened up for one's partner. One makes a sacrifice *of something* rather than *for someone*, and so one feels diminished rather than joyful. Fortunately, after a few weeks the you-scratch-my-back-and-I'll-scratch-yours approach to marriage usually results in a squabble. Then the couple remembers that being in love has more to do with making the beloved's desires one's own than with playing the role of the long-suffering spouse.

Making a spouse's hopes and desires one's own is not a magic spell for conjuring up a happy home. The partners will still have to negotiate over sinks filled with unwashed dishes, pungent cat boxes, or other unavoidable irritants of a shared life. Nevertheless, when genuine love triumphs over overt selfishness or self-absorbed self-abnegation, disputes can be approached with graciousness and even humor. The partners no longer find themselves playing out the unlikely scenario of calves demurring to one another at the trough. Instead, when we regard someone with wonder and hope that his or her potentialities be fulfilled, acting so as to further another's hopes and dreams is no longer a burden but a delight in itself.

Delight, not resentment or mutual indebtedness, is the basis of Christian charity. God wants us to be bound to him and to one another, not by a phoney and destructive solicitude, not by mutual neediness, but through loving wonder and the desire that those around us complete what God has begun in them. This is what it means to love others as God loves us. Loving as God loves and thereby living out the divine likeness means fostering and helping to complete God's creative work. Yet if this is the way in which God would have us deal with others, then it is also the way that God approaches us. If God wants us to love others without making them into extensions of ourselves, then God will not seek to absorb us. Instead, God wants to foster what is unique and good in each of us because it is in this way that his presence can be made manifest in creation. Viewed in this way, it is no more a paradox to say that oneness with God through love makes us even more ourselves than to say that a married man loves somebody other than himself. In desiring that his wife flourish, the husband simultaneously draws close to her and wonders at something distinct from himself. Similarly, as God draws near to us, we simultaneously discover our own unique parts in his unfolding plan for the cosmos.

Grafted into the Life of Christ

The Christian mystical tradition relies on three central metaphors in pointing to what it is like to experience union with God. Drawing on the experiences of farmers, married people, and on common experiences of seeing or understanding things, these metaphors aim at telling us what it is like to be both at one with God and, at the same time, most truly ourselves. As Saint John's gospel puts it, when at the prompting of the Holy Spirit we love as Christ loves, Christ dwells within us just as he abides in the Father (see John 14.1–16.33). When expressed in this way, the words register on the mind, and one gets a sense of what it might be like to experience the divine indwelling. Yet one is left standing a few steps away from the palpable experience of union with God. One learns something about *what* it is without quite grasping *how* it is. The point of traditional metaphors is to lead us past understanding into the experience of being one with God.

The most ancient of these metaphors come from the olive grove and vineyard. Explaining the Gentiles' connection to

God's promises to the Children of Israel, Saint Paul compared non-Jewish believers to wild olive twigs grafted onto the trunk of an old and reliable olive tree. "You, a wild olive shoot, were grafted in their place to share the rich root of the olive tree" (Romans 11.17). To put this idea in more modern terms, the heirs of God's promises to Abraham form a single organism with a single nurturing root even as the branches retain their unique genetic identities. In our little orchard behind the house, some of the dwarf trees contain as many as four distinct grafted-in components. The apple tree, for example, consists of a hearty root system grafted to a bit of material which will ensure the tree stays small grafted to a sturdy trunk itself grafted to the branches which will bear fruit. It is a single tree, but four different lives flourish within it.

As early as the second century Christian writers saw not only a metaphor for Christian unity in Paul's image of the olive tree but also an allegory for the individual Christian's union with Christ. Christ, they said, was the rich root, and we are the branches. In this way, union with Christ and our fellow Christians does not snuff out our personalities but, instead, allows us to become fruitful within the scope of a sustaining bond of love. The letter to the Ephesians also speaks of fruitfulness and incorporation into a larger organism through the theological metaphor of the mystical body of Christ (see Ephesians 1.1–24). Just as the good of the body is furthered by the unique functions of its parts, the beauty of communion of the saints resides in the uniqueness of its members.

In the gospel of Saint John, Christ uses the metaphor of grafting to explain how someone can be at one with God through love and yet fulfill his or her unique potentialities.

At the Last Supper Jesus tells his disciples, "I am the vine, you are the branches. Those who abide in me and I in them bear much fruit, because apart from me you can do nothing" (John 15.5). In the whole New Testament the Greek word translated as "branches" appears only in the fifteenth chapter of Saint John's Gospel. The word pointedly refers to the slips or cuttings grafted onto a grape vine, that is, to unique genetic material that comes to be woven into a single living system. Once again, we see distinct items sharing a common life. Our Lord takes the metaphor even further by identifying separate functions for himself and for those joined to him. Christ, like the stock and root system of a vine, sustains us, but, like a vine's lateral branches, it is our function to bear fruit. "Abide in me as I in you. Just as the branch cannot bear fruit by itself unless it abides in the vine, neither can you unless you abide in me" (John 15.4). Growing into the divine likeness means being grafted into the life of Christ, and it is his sustaining power that enables us to manifest God's fecundity in the midst of creation.

The Marriage of the Lamb

Another of the traditional metaphors for mystic union is marriage. Just as a husband and wife share a common life within which new life is fostered, as we become one with God we find ourselves participating in God's sustenance of creation and furthering his creative activity. This is why the climax of the book of Revelation comes not with the blood and thunder of the earlier chapters but with a wedding. The wedding of the Lamb, not the troubles delaying it, is what matters. Christ and the Church join together like a bride

and a bridegroom, and life in paradise is compared to the
wedding banquet.

> Hallelujah!
> For the Lord our God the Almighty reigns.
> Let us rejoice and exult and give him glory,
> for the marriage of the lamb has come,
> and his bride has made herself ready;
> to her it has been granted to be clothed
> with fine linen bright and pure. (Revelation 19.6–8)

The metaphor has its roots in the Old Testament.
Fundamentally, the Song of Solomon is a love poem. Some
of the rabbis who collected the writings of the Old
Testament chose to include the Song of Solomon because
they read it as an allegory for God's love for Israel. Other
rabbis argued that the Bible should reflect the whole of
human experience, and a bit of erotic poetry right in the
middle was just what the collection of holy writings needed.

Taking their cue from the book of Revelation's wedding
feast of the Lamb, ancient Christians like Origin (185–253)
found in the Song of Solomon not only an allegory for the
Church's oneness with Christ but also a metaphor for the
soul's union with God. Bernard of Clairvaux (1090–1153)
and other monks and nuns of the High Middle Ages continued the patristic tradition of reading the Song of Solomon as
an allegory for Christ's bond with the Church. Beyond this,
however, Bernard and his friends found in the old Hebrew
love poem a metaphor for Christ's pursuit of the soul and a
complex allegory illustrating the soul's journey into God.
Like a noble lady fallen on hard times, the soul has only a
dark beauty (Song of Solomon 1.5) until the lover recognizes

"a lily among brambles" (2.2). At first a wall stands between the couple, and they peer at one another through the lattice work (2.8–10). The lover invites the woman to come away with him, but by the time she reaches the door and throws it open he is gone. Then the bride begins a feverish search for the bridegroom. Similarly, having heard Christ's invitation the soul must go out seeking Christ, and, after a series of misadventures, Christ allows himself to be found. At this point in the poem the bride sings, "I am my beloved's and my beloved is mine" (6.3). In Bernard's allegory Christ and the soul become one, and the soul looks "with unveiled face upon the glory of the Bridegroom, [and is] changed into his likeness from one degree of glory to another, as by the Spirit of the Lord."[1]

Still, the root of all this is a poem about a couple falling in love. There is something shocking about speaking of God as one would speak of one's spouse, yet this is just what the tradition would have us do. Oneness with God is like the oneness of husband and wife because the same depth and familiarity are present in both relationships. At its best, marriage brings with it a sense of being well-understood and passionately cared for, and one discovers the same capacity for passionate understanding in oneself. Several years ago, a friend had just begun dating his future wife. They used to meet in the student union for coffee, and their late afternoon talks about schoolwork stretched into the dinner hour. I knew something was up and kidded my friend about

---

1. Bernard of Clairvaux, *Sermons on the Song of Songs*, 57.11, in *The Cistercian World: Monastic Writings of the Twelfth Century*, trans. Pauline Matarasso (London: Penguin Books, 1993), 77.

it. "It's like we've known each other all our lives," he said. Then I teased him some more, but I knew he was onto something. Union with God encompasses this same sort of delighted recognition; it is as if we had always known the divine presence.

We Will See Him as He Is

Among medieval mystics schooled in Greek philosophy, the most common metaphors for divine union were those dealing with knowledge and sense perception. In his book *On the Soul (De Anima)* Aristotle (384–322 BCE) taught that the human mind becomes, in some sense, one with what it thinks about or perceives. Aristotle, of course, did not mean that our minds become identical in all respects to those things outside them. After all, if our minds did become one and the same with what we thought about or perceived, we would get splitting headaches whenever we came into contact with especially large things. Instead, Aristotle held that we become one with things distinct from us by taking on their pattern. For example, my hearing a C-sharp played on a piano requires that the workings of my inner ear resonate at the same frequency as the piano string. When I become aware of what is going on in my ears, the sounding of the C-sharp and its being heard by me become a single event even though the piano string and the workings of my inner ear remain quite distinct. Similarly, while I can repeat the Pythagorean theorem or Newton's laws of motion to myself, I do not become Pythagoras or Sir Isaac Newton. In these cases, meaning is shared, not identity.

Meister Eckhart (1260–1329) developed a theology of mystical union that owed much to Aristotle's account of vision. Taking Christ's words "Blessed are the pure of heart, for they will see God" (Matthew 5.8) as his starting point, Eckhart taught that God and those who love him become one in the act of loving knowledge. In one of his sermons Eckhart puts it this way:

> As I made my way here today, I wondered how I might preach to you in such a way that you would be able to understand me. Then I thought of an analogy, and if you were able to understand it, you would understand both my meaning and the ground of all the sermons I have for so long been preaching. The analogy concerns the eye and a piece of wood. When my eye is open, it is an eye, but if it is closed it is the same eye. Nor does a block of wood decrease or increase in size by being looked at. Now listen carefully. If it now happens that my eye, which is one and simple in itself, is opened and directed towards the piece of wood in the act of seeing, then both remain what they are and yet both are so united through the act of seeing that we can truly say, 'eye-wood,' the wood is my eye. But if the wood had no material form and was as immaterial as the seeing of my eye, then we could truly say that the piece of wood and my eye share a single being in the act of seeing. If this is the case with material things, then how much more so with spiritual ones![2]

Just as the eye and the thing seen become one in the act of seeing, we can become one with God as we love and are loved by him. Nonetheless, we do not become God. He remains who he is, and we become more ourselves. Yet by

---

2. Meister Eckhart, "*Qui mihi ministra, me sequatur*" in *Meister Eckhart: Selected Writings*, trans. Oliver Davies (London: Penguin Books, 1994), 134–135.

loving and being loved by God we do become one with him in the act of loving itself. When we are at one with God through love, it is in much the same way that our eyes are at one with a sunrise in the act of seeing. Seeing the sunrise and the sunrise's being seen are one and the same thing. Our own love takes on the quality of divine love even as we remain quantitatively distinct from God.

Thomas Aquinas (1224–1273) taught that heaven consisted in the loving vision of God. As a careful reader of the Bible, Aquinas was captivated of these lines from the First Epistle of Saint John:

> Beloved, we are God's children now; what we will be has not yet been revealed. What we do know is this: when he is revealed, we will be like him, for we will see him as he is. (1 John 3.2)

As an intellectual, he wanted to understand them as fully as possible. Aquinas realized that Saint John did not have physical sight in mind. One cannot see God in the way that I see the last leeks and Brussels sprouts still standing in our garden. Seeing God as he is is much more like knowing and being known by him, provided that we understand "knowing" in the way we use the word when speaking of knowing those who are dear to us.

More than this, seeing or knowing God involves an experience of God which he initiates. "We love," says Saint John, "because he first loved us" (1 John 4.19). According to Saint Thomas, it is our way as human beings to learn about the existence of a creator by first discerning his imprint on the created order and then through his revelation of himself. We can discover that he exists but not who he is by examining creation, and through revelation we hear about God without coming to know him as we know our friends. In either case, we run up against Saint John's realization that "God is greater than our hearts" (1 John 3.20). We can learn that God exists by reading the book of nature, we can come to believe in the Trinity by reading scripture, but we cannot by our own devices know God himself.

Yet those trying to live as Christians seek God himself, not mere notions of God. Aquinas realizes that our ultimate communion with God must be a matter of sheer grace. In the *Summa Contra Gentiles* he puts it this way:

> Since human perfection lies in some manner of knowing God, and so that such noble creatures might not seem to have been created in vain, that is, not being able to attain their own purpose, human beings are given some way by which they might ascend to the knowledge of God.[3]

This way, as Aquinas puts it, is the elevation of the human mind by the light of grace. Since grace comes from outside our natures rather than from within us, we do not have to be particularly clever to be holy. One simply has to be ready to receive the gift.

Living the Transforming Union

In most respects, those deeply along in the transforming union look like the rest of us. They do not need to hive themselves off from the world, and if we find them behaving heroically it is only because the circumstances they find

---

3. Thomas Aquinas, *Summa Contra Gentiles* IV, 1 (my translation).

themselves in call for heroism. But all of them are deeply creative and prefer to be ethical rather than respectable. Such people always surprise us. One of our neighbors is a refined widow who sometimes asks me to translate Latin phrases because she claims her own Latin is rusty. I would guess that she is about eighty, but she makes a point of never mentioning her age. Her father was a minister and, later, a college president. She likes to smoke cigars when she is alone, and she lets a Vietnam veteran with a steel plate in his skull live in her tenant house. The veteran had been living under a bridge a few blocks from here, and our friend made a point of talking to him when she was out on her walks. When winter came, she invited him to live in her tenant house. That was seven years ago, and he has been there ever since. When it snows, he shovels most of the sidewalks in the neighborhood. I once asked her if she was conscious of taking a risk when she invited him to live there. All she told me was that she knew he was a good fellow. He is.

Another friend, a Trappist brother who entered the monastery when he was sixteen and who is now in his sixties seems always delighted by the world around him. Most recently, he has adopted a stretch of road near his monastery and walks it picking up cans and trash. He saves the cans and turns them in to be recycled. Half the money he makes he sends to Mother Teresa, and the other half he uses to buy margaritas when his abbot lets him go out for a Mexican dinner. When I received my Ph.D. he came to my graduation, and at a reception in the department offices he stood near the punch bowl charming the secretaries and feasting on cheese and crackers. When the reception ended he plucked a bouquet from its vase in the center of the table

and brought it back to the party at our house. It was disin-
terested theft; he thought that the flowers ought to be
enjoyed some more.

From time to time in this book I have alluded to the legend of Antony of Egypt. We saw how he sold his farm and
marched off into the wilderness to be alone with God and
have heard of his battles with the demons in the old pagan
tombs. These were episodes from the earlier portion of
Antony's life, when he was still trying to get clear of the preconceptions of his community and the limits of his own way
of seeing things. Antony remained faithful to the journey
and mellowed into a sweet and very old man who enjoyed
the company of the desert animals and receiving guests at
his hermitage. In his later years Antony supported himself
by braiding rope. One day while working inside his hut
Antony felt someone tugging at the other end of the rope he
was working on. Antony shuffled to the door and found a
monster human from the waist up and donkey from the hips
down holding the rope. Antony blessed the monster with
the sign of the cross and said, "I am Christ's servant. If you
are on a mission against me, here I am."[4] Antony's words
caused the creature to flee so quickly that it dropped dead
from a heart attack. Those living the transforming union
continually demonstrate the viability of the lamb when
confronted by the lion.

Divine union is not esoteric. It is not the bailiwick of a
few specialists locked away in hermitages or laboring in the
mission fields. No special knowledge and no special empa-
thy is necessary. It begins here and now with the desire to

---

4. Athanasius, *The Life of Antony*, trans Robert T. Meyer
(Westminster: The Newman Press, 1950), 65.

see creation as God sees it and to love it has he loves it. This second sight changes us, and that change launches a lifelong journey from intimations of the divine presence toward ever deeper participation in God's creative and sustaining work. Most of us are still like newly planted fruit trees. We have it in us to produce all sorts of wonderful things, and in time we will. But unlike fruit trees, there is no limit to our creative and sustaining activity because there are no limits to grace. We are capable of eternity, a timeless beginning in which our true natures unfold as God reveals himself to us. That begins now.

Also published by Continuum

William A. Meninger
THE PROCESS OF FORGIVENESS
"Going beyond Lewis Smedes's classic *Forgive and Forget*, Meninger makes abundant use of scripture to help readers understand forgiveness, and he recommends prayer to help them experience it."
—*Publishers Weekly Religion Bookline*

William A. Meninger
THE LOVING SEARCH FOR GOD
CONTEMPLATIVE PRAYER AND *THE CLOUD OF UNKNOWING*
"A powerful, even stunning job of explaining contemplative prayer...an excellent guide for anyone interested in deepening his or her Christian prayer life."
—*Publishers Weekly*

David G. Hackett
THE SILENT DIALOGUE
ZEN LETTERS TO A TRAPPIST ABBOT
"A clearly written and important book for anyone interested in Zen and Catholicism."
—*Library Journal*

Brian C. Taylor
SETTING THE GOSPEL FREE
EXPERIENTIAL FAITH AND CONTEMPLATIVE PRACTICE
"An ideal example of the new, but very old synthesis that always renews Christianity from the bottom up and from the inside out. Brian Taylor's reaching is clear, faith-filled, and grounded in centuries of experience."
—Richard Rohr, O.F.M.

Nan C. Merrill
PSALMS FOR PRAYING
AN INVITATION TO WHOLENESS
"[Merrill] has reworked the *Book of Psalms* in a loving, contemplative manner....Merrill's psalms evoke that deep sense of reverence and soul-stirring dialogue with the divine."

—Library Journal

THE COMPLETE BOOK OF CHRISTIAN PRAYER
A beautifully arranged treasury of 1200 classic and contemporary prayers from over 560 authors and sources, more than half of whom are from this century.

Lauren Glen Dunlap and Kathleen Frugé-Brown
AND I, FRANCIS
THE LIFE OF FRANCIS OF ASSISI IN WORD AND IMAGE
"One of the most breathtaking books on the subject....The artwork is strong, conveying a sense of the mystical, making for a beautiful book that will remain for a long, long time in the minds and hearts of readers." *—Publishers Weekly*

Kevin M. Cronin, Editor
A FRIAR'S JOY
MAGIC MOMENTS FROM REAL LIFE
"The most unputdownable book of 1996....Each story is a winner, unique, like no other tale, real as the rustle of a brown habit, deep as the cowl into which a friar places missives." *—National Catholic Reporter*